UNIVERSAL LIFE CHURCH
P.O. BOX 150
TILTON, N.H. 03276
(603) 286-8191

The Prism of Lyra

An Exploration of Human Galactic Heritage

•Lyssa Royal and Keith Priest•

A Royal Priest Research Book

Published by Light Technology and Royal Priest Research Press

To contact the authors:
Royal Priest Research
Lyssa Royal and Keith Priest
Post Office Box 10546
Sedona, Arizona 86336

Cover Art and Chapter Illustrations:
Michael Z. Tyree
Post Office Box 405
Clarkdale, Arizona 86324

Printed in the United States of America by Mission Possible Commerical Printing, P.O. Box 1495, Sedona, AZ 86336.

To the children of Lyra scattered throughout the galaxy near and far...may you remember your heritage.

"I am a child of Earth and starry Heaven;
But my race is of Heaven alone.
This ye know yourselves..."

—Translated from the Petelia
Plate
Orphic Initiates, 200-400 B.C.

Acknowledgements

This manuscript came about mostly because it was the kind of book we have been searching for for several years. Since it wasn't available, we wrote it! We thank all those who also searched and then lovingly inspired us to create it.

We thank channel Darryl Anka (and Bashar) for providing the initial inspiration starting in 1985 to begin the search for this complex yet intriguing information. The integrity he possesses and the quality of his channeling inspired our confidence that this information could be reliably obtained.

We thank channel Robert Shapiro, for providing some unique and elusive information regarding the Zeta Reticuli and the negative Sirians. Robert has the courage to tackle areas as a channel that many individuals are not willing to approach.

We thank Barbara Hand Clow at Bear and Company, for offering valuable feedback and encouragement during revisions of the manuscript. Her enthusiastic responses to our work helped perpetuate our momentum and focus us at the moments we valued it most.

We thank Michael Z. Tyree for his sharp intuitive sense in creating artwork that expresses the deep symbolism of this information.

We send love and thanks to the Thursday Evening Group for sitting through eight weeks of Sedona's record-breaking heat in order to delve more deeply into the extraterrestrial issue by utilizing the channeling process of Lyssa Royal.

We thank Jeannine Calaba for her detailed and insightful critique of the first draft. Her love, friendship and support has been invaluable to this project.

We thank Beth Pierson for her surprisingly meticulous proofreading and valuable feedback on the material. She delivered all that we asked for, and some that we didn't!

We thank Margaret Pinyan for her highly professional editing, proofreading, and typesetting.

We thank Stacey Vornbrock for pointing out awkwardness and offering suggestions on a most difficult section of the book...and for the coconut cake.

Appreciation goes to Julie Rapkin for saying "It's wonderful!"

Many thanks to Steve and Rita Hansen for their support and technical help during the last chaotic weeks of publication!

Deepest thanks to O'Ryin Swanson and the Light Technology staff for their care and professionalism in the entire printing process.

Note To Readers

Royal Priest Research plans subsequent books delving more deeply into this information. If you have questions or comments on the material please correspond with us. Your questions will be logged and used for a second volume of this work.

Special Note: We are gathering data on dreams and waking experiences concerning extraterrestrial interactions, especially dreams/experiences regarding the Orion conflict. If you have an experience you would like to share please contact:

Royal Priest Research
P.O. Box 10546
Sedona, Arizona 86336

Table of Contents

Preface

*"It was not the mixture, O men, of blood and breath
that made the beginning and substance of your souls,
though your earthborn and mortal body is framed of
those things. But your soul has come hither from
another place."*

—Empedocles

From the earliest days in Earth's recorded history, there has been a bittersweet emotion that wells up within us as we gaze into the expanse of the night sky. Some of us long for the day when the human race can travel beyond the stars. Is it really a hope for the future rather than just a remembrance of our past?

The human consciousness has intricacies that still remain unexplored. What stirs us to push evolution to its limits? What drives us to create dissension between the races on our planet? Perhaps it is possible that we are playing out a cosmic drama and have only temporarily forgotten the script. We know that what one country or race does upon the Earth affects another. This idea may also spread outward into the universe. Perhaps what we do here affects countless other civilizations on other planets. Could we really be that linked together?

The information presented in this book is a compilation of years of insights, deductive reasoning, and channeling. Meticulous cross referencing of various channels has been conducted (including the work of co-author Lyssa Royal), as well as research into a number of respected anthropological and metaphysical works. The reader may consider these ideas to be literal or symbolic, for the story is the same. There is no claim that this is the ultimate truth of our galactic family's emergence into this reality. If it works for you, use the insights given here as a catalyst for your own growth. If not, perhaps it can lead you one step closer to your own personal truth.

One of the most important ideas to accelerate the human potential is the allowance of all truths to be a manifestation of the One Truth, whatever it may be. Through this allowance emerges unification. If nothing else, let this book be fun to read, interesting, and stimulating to your imagination. Your belief is certainly not required—but your willingness to be an explorer is!

This is an introductory book. An extensive glossary has been created at the end of the material for any unfamiliar terms that may have been used. Each chapter represents a different facet of an intricate tapestry and how the tapestry affects Earth. Through many discussions, the information has been honed down into a framework that will introduce the reader to a cast of characters. The cast is not complete. There are countless other members and dramas being played out throughout our universe. These characters have emerged as the ones who seem to matter most to the human drama here on Earth.

There are certain assumptions carried throughout the material that are a foundation for the rest of the information. One of these is the idea of reincarnation and the infinite nature of consciousness. It is not necessary to embrace this concept in order to grasp the material, but it will allow the reader a more expanded view of the bigger picture.

Another assumption presented is the idea that each being possesses a higher awareness. It is purported that regardless of the level of existence a being has chosen for a given lifetime, it retains an awareness (conscious or subconscious) of its connection to the Whole and its divine identity. This concept connects us with the idea that it is *we and we alone* who control our destinies. Therefore, evolution is in our own hands.

Throughout the entire book the assumption will also be carried that the "Whole," or the integrated mass consciousness of our galactic family, has always existed. For the purposes of the information presented, there will need to be some set parameters. These parameters will allegorically refer to the "beginning" of the story as being the *Dimensional Infusion* and the "end" as the *Integration.*

In may cases labels have been used to denote places or people (such as Sirius, or Sirians). In general, these labels are fluid, more denoting a *realm* or *vibrational awareness* than a fixed idea. In a case such as Lyra, for example, the possibility is respected that the very stars spoken of have become black holes and white holes many times over. Therefore, these can be spoken of as *ideas* rather than concrete points in time and space. These ideas carry weight; this is quite apparent in our legends that give importance to other star systems. The Dogon tribe legends, the Sumerian Texts, and the ancient Egyptian writings all claim contact with beings from other star systems. These legends must come from *somewhere.* Though their language and contemporary style of expression differ slightly, the consistency of their content is beyond argument.

Information about the past of the human race can enrich our lives *here* on Earth. If we are to truly transform, it will be through the infusing of awareness onto our world, *not* using the awareness to escape from our responsibilities as citizens of Earth and the Galactic Family.

Note: Read the footnotes and the glossary!

1

Dimensional Infusion

"With its celestial keys,
Its chords of air, its frets of fire,
The Samian's great Aeolian Lyre,
Rising through all its sevenfold bars,
From Earth unto the fixed stars."

—Longfellow on Lyra
from *Occultation of Orion*

All consciousness and energy was once fused into an integrated whole. This Whole was aware of aspects of itself, but in a different way from individualized consciousness. In Earth's present development the self is recognized first, then society, and finally the Whole, All That Is, or God. Separation is still created. This separation from the Source is an illusion. This illusion is a tool that provides the Whole with all the necessary lessons and challenges it needs to experience in order to reintegrate back into the Source.

Before this fragmentation from the Source, the Whole existed in another octave of dimensional reality. From this realm of unification, portions of All That Is wondered what it would be like to fragment and temporarily forget integrated existence. The force of this thought on such a mass level began to create a fragmentation. The illusion created from this fragmentation would be a challenging forgetfulness in which consciousness would need to create (from its own divine nature) the remembrance to once again unite.

What has been termed "creation" is indeed this fragmentation, or, more descriptively, the *Dimensional Infusion.* The Whole's initial curiosity about a fragmented existence actually *created* the reality itself. It required a shift in perspective, focus, or frequency. As part of the Whole, aspects of the Galactic Family were partially responsible for laying out the blueprint that was to guide their development. Therefore, the statement "we are God" actually has viable meaning.

The blueprint that was laid out contained many different ideas. It first held the notion that polarity and fragmentation would be the norm. The encoding in the blueprint provided the option of Free Will on the part of each fragment or soul. The challenge was in remembering that each consciousness possessed it. The more Free Will is used, the more divine memory is invoked. When faced with a polarized reality, Free Will becomes the liberator. When a soul forgets it possesses Free Will, the lessons become much more challenging, yet quite rewarding.

Another idea present in this chosen blueprint was that fragments of the Whole would be entirely responsible for its actions during this state of amnesia. Whether or not it was remembered, every action taken would generate a response from the universe. Some have called this karma; however, it is much more than "an eye for an eye." Instead of punishments for negative behavior, there is always the option of expanding one's awareness. Therefore, in a sense, wisdom erases karma.

Though this may sound like the rules for some kind of cruel cosmic game, the outcome has already been decided. With this in mind, it is not necessarily the destination that counts but the journey along the way. It is literally *how* the game is played.

Another blueprint that was agreed to was an etherically generated code built into the fabric of the universal tapestry. This code would allow bipedal, carbon-based humanoid forms to be the normal, naturally developing vehicle for the incarnation of human-type consciousness on planetary structures. This code exists on meta-atomic levels that science is just beginning to learn to measure. The symbology of polarity plays out in the human body form. The Earth human is symmetrical, with two arms, two legs, two eyes, ears, etc. The body is joined into a whole by a torso and a head.

It was also decided that during the evolutionary development of humanoid forms (within the Earth's galactic family) that the male and female polarities would manifest in separate but complimentary body types. This serves as a reminder that in order to create, polarities must always be joined or integrated. The notion is widely held that an individual has a tendency to feel most "at One" when he/she is joined with another in love.

What was the actual process of the Dimensional Infusion? There exists within the time/space fabric of the constellation Lyra what can be called a white hole.[1] Compare this white hole to a prism. In passing a beam of light through a prism, one gets a spectrum of light fragmented into seven visible color frequencies. When a portion of the Whole passed through the *Prism of Lyra* (the white hole), consciousness was fragmented into seven vibratory frequencies that represent the mass consciousness of Earth's galactic family. Each fragment became conscious on all of these different frequencies or densities. Frequencies were previously experienced as being integrated into the Whole (like white light). When this portion of the Whole passed through the prism, it manifested as seven aware frequencies. Consciousness also fragmented "away" from each other, as the "Big Bang" theory symbolically suggests. The illusion thus arose that each fragment was very, very alone.

The Whole understood that the purpose of this experience was to learn to reintegrate from a point of separation. But how? As individual souls or in groups the fragments sought out the universe that was just created. The Dimensional Infusion not only created a consciousness fragmentation, but it also created the stars, planets, gases, and molecules that make up physical reality. However, physical reality represents only a few of the energy frequencies that emerged from the fragmentation.

As science has discovered, matter is densified energy vibrating at a specific rate. Every aspect of the universe is made up of energy. In Earth technology it has not yet been discovered how to measure certain portions of reality. If technology possessed this ability, an infinite number of gateways into time, space and dimension would be seen. For the time being, the seven frequency levels that Earth's galactic family fragmented into by passing through the Prism of Lyra will be explored. From this point forward the term "density" will be used in reference to these frequency levels.[2]

FIRST DENSITY: **Awareness as a point; Physical matter.**

This frequency level is the most basic. It provides the matter and energy for the creation of atoms and molecules. The basic life forms of mineral and water, for example, are all operating from first-density frequency. Humans possess this frequency within as well. It makes up the basic genetic codes.

SECOND DENSITY: **Awareness as a line; Biological matter; Development of group or species identity.**

The consciousness expressed by second-density vibration does not possess self-awareness (or ego). Most species within the plant and animal kingdoms exist here; however, their placement in density depends upon many additional factors, including the presence or absence of ego.

THIRD DENSITY: **Volumetric awareness; Ego; Loss of group identity, development of individual identity; Ability to remember past and cognize the future while retaining present awareness.**

This is the density where human beings emerge. It is a vibration that creates the illusion of separation and thus a challenge toward awakening. Presently humanity is going through a transition period into fourth-density reality which can account for the many rapid changes the human race is undergoing. Cetaceans (dolphins and whales) presently exist simultaneously in third and fourth densities and are transitioning out of third along with humanity. The consciousness of primates exists in third density as well. This is becoming increasingly apparent, as one begins to observe them displaying several characteristics that were once thought of as indigenous only to humans (such as language acquisition and pathological behavior). This is the frequency that expresses the most separation from the Whole. It is from here that many lessons about integration are learned. This is the most intense of all levels in its cultivation of growth within the Self.

FOURTH DENSITY: **Containment of volumetric awareness; Superconsciousness; Reintegration of group identity without loss of ego identity; As vibration in-**

creases, perception of past, present, and future become more fluid along with the ability to interface with multidimensional and multidensity realities; Negatively oriented consciousness becomes more difficult to maintain.

Presently on Earth, fourth-density reality is overlapping third. In humanity's case, this can account for the increased desire for unity, peace, and unconditional love as opposed to the illusion of separation that characterizes third density. The vibratory rate of one's reality is stepped up, and therefore one may be faced with personal issues in a much more rapid and intense way. It is easy to see how this is coming into play with the thousands of individuals upon Earth who are in therapy, in substance-abuse programs, and engaging in humanistic efforts to better the planet. This is the frequency of responsibility. This is the frequency when one begins to remember the encoding of Free Will. This is the last frequency where physical bodies are the vehicles for the expression of consciousness. Hence many civilizations choose to spend long periods of time within this density.

(Note: There is no clear-cut distinction when transitioning from fifth to sixth and sixth to seventh densities. Because these densities are not physically oriented, there is much blending in these transitions.)

FIFTH DENSITY: Experiential awareness of "I" as a group identity; Not bound by linear time.

In this density sentient consciousness begin to awaken to its heritage. This is the density of wisdom. As one awakens the wisdom within, they very often want to share it with those who are still focused in the lower densities. Many from this realm choose to become guides for others. A fifth-density being merges with its family of consciousness ("oversoul" or "higher self," if you will) and begins to remember. This is the first density in which a nonphysical orientation is experienced.

SIXTH DENSITY: **Awareness as the dimension itself.**

This has often been called the "Christ Consciousness" in that it displays a frequency level equal to that of the Christ or Buddha. From this frequency a total remembrance occurs, and one begins taking responsibility for the Whole rather than the Self. The process of progressing the Self and progressing the Whole become one and the same.

SEVENTH DENSITY: **Awareness as the multidimensional experience; Group-matrix identity (Social Memory Complex).**

This is the frequency of total oneness or integration. Those who vibrate to this frequency are merged in identity and become a mass-conscious whole. They magnetize those in other frequencies and provide the current for the natural flow toward integration. Once the seventh density beings reach critical mass, they will progress through the Prism of Lyra (from our point of view it will then be a black-hole exit point) and reach the next octave, where another adventure awaits.

It is important to note that as portions of the Whole fragmented through the Prism of Lyra, each consciousness retained awareness on *all* density levels. However, part of the forgetfulness remained. From most highly focused density levels (such as third and portions of fourth), an unawareness may occur concerning the coexistence of other levels. As integration occurs, one becomes aware of these other aspects.

The microcosm always reflects the macrocosm. This is visible in the "coincidence" of how atomic structure mirrors the structure of a solar system. It is the same with the fragmentation of portions of the Whole into individual beings or soul groups. When one incarnates into a physical body, it can be likened to a mini-passage through the Prism of Lyra.

The process of soul fragmentation as one incarnates physically can be likened somewhat to Freud's id, ego, and super-ego theories. As a fetus, the soul demonstrates a first-density consciousness. At that point, one is aware of itself as intricately connected to the environment. Physically, one is a mass of DNA codes with the potential to become a conscious human being. Since Freud did not take his hypothesis into prenatal development, there is no correlation. If he were to create a label that describes the fetus' relationship to its environment, then it would be a first-density description.

When the child is between birth and two years old, he/she begins to demonstrate second-density consciousness. A separation begins to be perceived between itself and the environment and its desires become externalized. There is still somewhat of an egocentric point of view, which correlates this developmental level with the id. What distinguishes a child's second-density orientation from third density is the lack of a distinct ability to differentiate between itself and the environment.

From approximately the second year of life onward, third-density consciousness becomes the primary framework demonstrated. This is the development of the ego and the awareness of the child as a separate individual. These are crucial formative years; one can see that if development is disrupted (such as through abuse) the personality can fragment and perhaps create dysfunction later in life. Many individuals retain this third-density consciousness orientation of ego throughout their entire lives.

The development of the superego, or higher awareness, is a typical fourth-density trait. Humans have the option to develop this aspect of themselves. This is a reintegration of the fragmentation of personality that occurs through the birth process, as well as integration on a spiritual level. As the human race begins to move more solidly into fourth-density consciousness, it is suspected that this personality fragmentation process will become less apparent, and perhaps children will begin displaying fourth-density characteristics earlier in their development and retain them throughout their lives.

In childhood one must learn how to adapt and integrate into a workable framework. If one cannot do this (such as in the instance of child abuse) psychological disorders will very often be displayed when adulthood is reached. Pathologies such as Multiple Personality Disorder can occur because the natural third-density personality integration process did not occur during childhood. Some extraterrestrial civilizations have learned to detect and transmute the seeds of pathological disorders during childhood, and therefore have no incidence of adult pathologies.

If it is understood that no matter how far an individual fragments (either on a soul level or in the personality), and that the way back home is always through integration, he/she will never lose sight of the goal. In this case, we *can* go home again.

---

[1]A focus of intense light and energy. In this case, a birthplace.

[2]See Glossary of Terms for the differences between "density" and "dimension."

2

Creation of the Galactic Family

"I am Ra, from whom time began.
I am the hub of a wheel,
A day star hovering over an endless sea.
I am not the harvest; I am the seed.
I am not the Lyre; I am the song.
I will not pass away."

—Egyptian Book of the Dead
Ellis Translation

In passing through the Prism of Lyra, the first fragmentation created a group of beings that can be called the Founders.[1] The Founders embodied the group consciousness of what eventually became humankind. They can project to a very high level of fourth density, but their natural state is nonphysical. In splitting off from the portion of the Whole that passed through the Prism of Lyra, they still retained a memory, if somewhat dreamlike, of the idea of integration and the purpose of the fragmentation. It is they who orchestrate humankind's evolution. They play the roles of the parent archetype, in male and female polarity balance.

The Founders became aware of the blueprint that was chosen as they fragmented from the Whole. From this blueprint they knew that "children" carry the encodings of the "parents." Since they played the parents' role, it was their responsibility to influence the growth of the new consciousness about to be created. In doing this they *became* the blueprint, began to understand and live it, knowing that this would encode future fragments.

The Founders began to understand the natural energy patterns of the polarized reality just created. It became obvious to them that the newly fragmented group consciousness interfaces with specific realities (i.e. densities) within three main points: (1) A point of pure positivity; (2) A point of pure negativity; (3) The integrative point of the two. All interactions occur within the lines that connect each point, with very few aspects of consciousness existing within the points of purity. This realization inspired them to understand a paradigm of polarized reality, which was something exciting and new to their understanding. The paradigm, as it emerged for them, is shown below in a two-dimensional diagram.

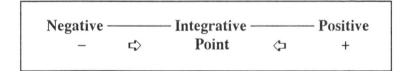

As they pondered the paradigm they began to understand the mechanics of how the fragmented consciousness would once again merge back through the Prism of Lyra. The linear model above can be changed to bring about the triadic relationship of the template. This is shown below.

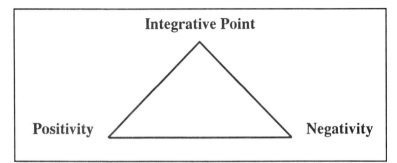

This triad represents the probabilities of the integrative process. Civilizations naturally move randomly (according to the laws of chaos) within the triadic template until a balance of energy is reached.

If a civilization or consciousness chooses integration (the willingness to grow from both polarities), they will naturally move toward the integrative point, fueled by the momentum of both polarities. This can be viewed as an allowing form of integration. If, on the other hand, a civilization or individual refuses integration, the template expands to accommodate their denial of the opposite polarity. The expanded template will not be outlined here at the present time.

When they believed they were ready, the Founders began another fragmentation. Just as a portion of the Whole became curious and created this realm from its thoughts, the Founders emulated their "parents" and exerted thought energy to create a fragmentation of themselves. This fragmentation occurred far and wide; individualized consciousness sprang from the Founders' group awareness and began to explore the universe. Because of this fragmentation, every being existing in the galactic family presented here is part of the Founders.

There are an infinite number of fragments and explorational journeys. Some of these fragments grew into civilizations that have played a part in the development of Earth. Some of those who have a reference point in Earth's known reality will be explored in the chapters ahead.

When the Founders fragmented, some allowed their energy to densify sufficiently in order to enter a physical reality. The Founders had already chosen planets that could support humanoid life. Then they gently guided these fragments into a physical, third- or fourth-density existence. After time had passed, the fragments became more accustomed to physical existence, and assistance from the Founders (who still existed in smaller numbers) became less needed.

The first area to be eventually colonized after the Founders' fragmentation was in the general vicinity of the Lyra constellation. Most of the galactic family that has genetic connections to Earth has roots in the Lyran system. It was there that the first attempt at integration occurred. The Founders thought that it would be easy and predictable; instead, humanoid lifeforms spread outward exponentially until a very intricate tapestry was woven. The threads of the tapestry began to become tangled until eventually the origins of the thread became lost in the colorful maze of the tapestry's design.

The following are the main characters displayed in this tapestry from the perspective of Earth:

Lyra: The general area of the "birth"of the humanoid race. The term "Lyra" can also denote the symbolic feminine polarity manifestation within the Lyran system.

Vega: A star within the constellation of Lyra that housed the symbolic incarnation of the masculine polarity within the Lyran system.

Apex Planet: A planet within the Lyran system which was the first attempt at creating an integrated society.

Sirius: A trinary star group, it is known in Earth mythology as the Dog Star. Sirius was one of the first areas to be colonized by beings from the Lyran star group. Sirius embodied the energy of the triadic template and perpetuated the drive toward integration. There is a large variety of consciousness types that incarnate in this system.

Orion: This is the main "battleground" for the challenge of polarity integration, seeded from Sirius as well as Lyra. There is a direct connection with Earth, as explored in later chapters.

Pleiades: Colonized by Lyran offshoots, this group is Earth's main genetic connection from extraterrestrial sources.

Arcturus: An archetype or future-self ideal of Earth, Arcturus assists in healing personal and planetary consciousness. Its vibration, primarily sixth density, has been attributed to the angelic kingdom.

Zeta Reticuli: This civilization is intimately connected with Earth. The Reticuli are the primary group instigating abductions (or more accurately called "temporary detainments" since this group always returns the abductee). More will be said about this group in later chapters.

Though some of these civilizations overlap each other in time and may not appear linear, below is a linear translation of the progression of various cultures in comparison to each other.

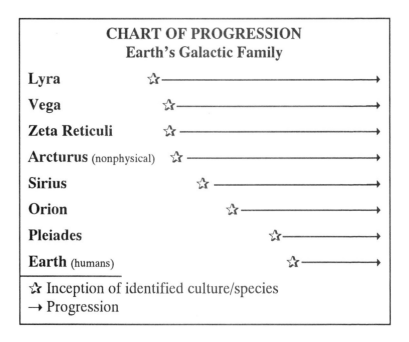

CHART OF PROGRESSION
Earth's Galactic Family

Lyra	☆———————————————————→
Vega	☆———————————————————→
Zeta Reticuli	☆ ——————————————————→
Arcturus (nonphysical)	☆ —————————————————→
Sirius	☆ ————————————————→
Orion	☆ —————————————→
Pleiades	☆—————————————→
Earth (humans)	☆—————————→

☆ Inception of identified culture/species
→ Progression

Discussion

Once one recovers from the initial shock of the idea that extraterrestrials had something to do with Earth's heritage, it really seems like a very logical explanation. Why would the human race egotistically believe that it alone is responsible for Earth's genetic past? Upon Earth, races have "discovered" new races and have begun integrating with them. Perhaps before this occurred, these races never knew the others existed. This model can hold true for the universe as well as planet Earth. How many more ancient drawings of rocketships and their pilots need to be found before humans can break through the fears about discovering Earth's past?

The most obvious question is this: If the extraterrestrials are out there, why don't they show themselves? An answer can be found in humanity's approach to anthropological studies upon Earth. Scientists do not go marching right in to a "primitive" culture waving their cameras and equipment. These types of cultural assimilations sometimes take them decades to accomplish. In its own eyes, humanity may seem "civilized" enough. However, to a race that has achieved space travel and perhaps even global unity, humanity may seem primitive indeed. Perhaps they are waiting, hiding in the bushes, allowing only a few humans to see them until the signal goes out to the whole of society that they are not a threat.

What if the signal that they are there never goes out to society? What if humanity continues to ignore the evidence, hoping it will all go away? To many of the extraterrestrials, this seems to be the case. All nonthreatening methods seem to have been unsuccessful thus far. The primary game plan over the last few decades appears to be much more profound in its potential to awaken humanity. Some of Earth's visitors are now using fear. At times society is so quick to validate negativity rather than positivity that humanity's own framework may now begin to be used to assimilate Earth to its previously denied reality. Fear awakens—rather rudely at that. Hence a reasoning behind the growing observation of extraterrestrial abduction experiences.

At humanity's level of development, a model for the natural evolution of a planet has not yet been formulated. It seems obvious that a civilization would not be able to reach the cosmos and the folding of space/time dimensions if it cannot resolve its conflicts on a planetary level. The expansion of consciousness required for such a leap may be dependent upon the unified whole. If the whole is not integrated and balanced, attempts may be fruitless. Humanity may be experiencing this limitation now, with so many unsuccessful space-launch attempts as well as space program budget restrictions. Earth may just not be ready. Humanity wants to reach for the stars but very often cannot even reach for the hand of its neighbor.

The extraterrestrial connection is important, but what is even more important is developing a global perspective. Expansion will come from action—the claiming of responsibility for Earth by humanity itself. The extraterrestrials will not intervene to clean up humanity's mess. Earth is entering adulthood and has been kicked out of the nest. It would serve humanity to release its victimhood, claim its divine birthright, and *create* heaven on Earth. The extraterrestrials can only remind humanity of its unlimited potential. Their communication (and our awareness of Earth's heritage) can be likened to a dangling carrot. If the human race wants that carrot, perhaps it must do what needs to be done to get it—unify and integrate.

1 Other terms such as the Watchers, Reflectors, and Seeders are equally appropriate.

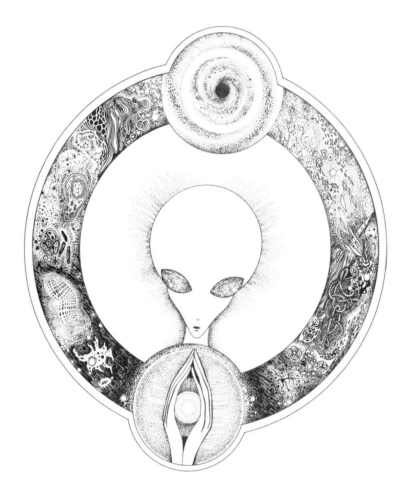

3

The Womb of Lyra

"When I became," said he, "the becoming became.
I have become the becoming.
I am one seeing myself, divided.
I am two and four and eight.
I am the universe in diversity.
I am my transformations.
This is my coming together.
Here are my selves become one."

—*Egyptian Book of the Dead*
Ellis Translation

From the point of view of a reality that can be perceived by physical beings, the form of the Founders has two arms, two legs, a head, and a torso. They possess large, inquisitive eyes as a symbolic representation of their desire for knowledge and of the ancient memory that they carry within them. Physical beings would view them as insectlike, very tall, and having long, graceful limbs. Third-density humans can perceive them if they enter an accelerated version of fourth density. Interactions with them are usually able to occur in an altered state. From this state they appear etheric and dreamlike.[1]

Having fragmented their consciousness further, the Founders began solidifying energy into matter to create a prototype physical race for the majority of humanoid consciousness to incarnate into. On meta-atomic levels, organizational codes exist that create a consistent humanoid-type body in a carbon-based environment as the vehicle for physical representation of consciousness.[2] The Founders used this naturally occurring code to assist them in creating versions of themselves in both physical and nonphysical states. This form symbolically reflected the aspects of the polarized universe they had entered into. Again, it is representative of the idea that "parents" create "children" in their own image.

The Founders are the energetic grandparents of the human race. It was their desire to manifest different dimensional aspects of themselves. This would produce root forms of life which would facilitate the process of creating diversity within the new reality that was just born. They are both the Source and the prototype.

As they emerged into this light form through the densification of energy, they became aware that all life will once again evolve back into the Founders and then into the Source. Consciousness will scatter and fragment, sometimes beyond recognition; but it will evolve back into the Source *physically*, as well as mentally, emotionally, and spiritually.

Thus the Founders began the next step of the fragmentation process. Their first action was to begin making the plans necessary to spread life throughout the Lyran system. They were aware that over time the life forms would naturally gravitate into planetary civilizations by means of attraction.

Planets were chosen within the Lyran star group to house these new races. As these planets naturally began to develop primate life, the Founders seeded these developing primates with plasmic energy[3] on meta-atomic levels within their DNA structure. This occurred over many generations until the primates/humanoids possessed the genetics necessary to sustain the higher vibrations of third-density consciousness. With slight alterations the incarnation process was soon to begin on several planetary bodies.

The Founders fragmented themselves further in order to release the consciousness necessary to incarnate on these planets. As this fragmentation occurred, each consciousness was magnetized to a specific planet where the vibrations were more compatible with the individual fragment.

As expressed in the previous chapter, the basic template of the consciousness that fragmented through the Prism of Lyra can be considered a triad. It represents one polarity, its opposite, and the integrative point. The Founders observed this natural flow of energy emerging in the base species that were developing. These different planetary groups were initially homogeneous, not yet manifesting any single aspect of the template in an obvious way.

As time went on and interactions between individuals and groups increased, many groups polarized into either negative or positive orientations.[4] Some groups began to display varying degrees of integration. This scenario was expected by the Founders. However, the process began to take on a life of its own. As the process grew exponentially, the Founders began to see the infinite reflections of the Whole, and to some extent it became overwhelming to them.

As these groups evolved and achieved space travel, they exposed themselves to the development of other planetary groups in the area. Cultures began to mix and grow. New philosophies were born. For a period of time the Lyran races rapidly developed advanced technology, expansive

philosophy, and strong social development due to the interactions between these planetary cultures. Then the dynamics
of the template began to be displayed.

Polarities began to solidify, generating their own polarization that continued exponentially in turn. Negative polarities
began splitting and manifesting their own negative/positive
poles. Positive poles did the same. The feminine expressed
its masculine, and the masculine expressed its feminine.
Polarities exploded like viruses within the previously blos-
soming civilization.

The simple set of mirrors that the Founders had created
shattered into infinite fragments. They had lost direct contact
with many of the genetic windows (physical beings) that they
had created. The physical beings had now taken on a life of
their own, although the original programs continued to be an
underlying factor influencing their development.

The first group to develop as a specific non-Lyran species
was the Vegan civilization.[5] They formed a highly distinc-
tive philosophy and spiritual orientation and began to isolate
themselves from the Lyran races. They were initially a
negatively oriented civilization, expressed as the negative
pole of Lyra because they had adopted a philosophy of service
to self (contraction). Lyra itself may be considered the positive pole because all other civilizations were "born" out of it
(expansion).

As time passed, friction grew between the people of the
Lyran races and the Vegan civilizations. Neither civilization
was progressing in an integrative way. Both possessed within
themselves the conflict of polarity. Neither group was right
or wrong; they all played out the same ideas, only from a
different perspective. They just could not understand how to
balance their energies. Polarization continued to grow ex-

ponentially as they grappled with their relationships between their civilizations and themselves.

A third civilizations began to emerge from the Lyran races. Because this planet was the apex of a symbolic triangle of integration (playing out both negative and positive polarities), it can be called the Apex planet during this stage of its development. Later, it becomes a much more intricate piece of this galactic puzzle.

The Apex planet began its civilization by drawing in characteristics from both the Lyra and Vega polarities. Genetically they were a mixture. Within their race diversity was even more widespread than upon our present Earth. There were dark- and light-skinned people, pacifists and conquerors, artists, musicians, and soldiers. Even in comparison to our Earth race, they did not coexist peacefully at all. Separation began occurring in the culture until the entire planet was engulfed in the friction of polarity. No resolution was in sight. The future of this Apex planet seemed hopeless—they eventually allowed pollution and weaponry to nearly destroy their world.

When opposite polarities are forced, not integrated, they cause fusion. This fusion manifested on the Apex world as nuclear war. A small number of inhabitants secured themselves underground, but the remainder perished from their own inability to integrate. What occurred on a planetary scale was quite interesting. From a point of observation in space, it appeared that the planet destroyed itself. From the point of view of the survivors who went underground, they were very much alive. As a result of their nuclear explosions their planet was eventually propelled into an alternate dimension.

After the cataclysm, radiation upon their world remained quite high which forced them to stay underground. Once they recovered from their emotional shock, it became time to pick up the shattered pieces of their lives. Their development and their amazing transformation will be explored in further chapters, for they play a vital role not only in the transformation of planet Earth but of the galactic family and the Founders as well.

Meanwhile, Lyra and Vega were continuing with their development. Groups of Lyrans wished to remove themselves from the friction with Vega and sought out many other areas to colonize. Groups of Vegans also escaped their planet's conflicts and founded a number of civilizations including Altair. Gone were the clear-cut lines of traceable philosophic and genetic history. Humanity was spreading quickly, carrying with it the seeds of experience and polarity. The goal was always buried deep within the souls of each being and it gently nudged them on. The goal was, and still is, integration.

It is apparent that the beginnings of the entrance into polarity by the Founders was not easy. They had created an equation that they expected would conclude according to their calculations. As with the new science of chaos, the movement of energy between these three civilizations (Lyra, Vega, and Apex) became unpredictable to the Founders. The entire galactic family could only wait and watch, knowing that in chaos there is order—divine order.

These early lessons have been imprinted into humanity's etheric memory as a reminder of all that it has been and all that it can become. Humanity is never alone in this struggle. The Founders still wait silently. They exist not only "out there" but also within the soul of humanity as its most basic archetype. The cycle of life and existence is merely a circle; the beginning and end are the same. When humanity feels the call of evolution, it is the Founders whispering through

the expanse of time and dimension. They are a part of
humankind speaking to itself. Perhaps it is time to listen.

---

[1]In dream symbology, the Founders may translate into figures like
large such as praying mantises, walking sticks, and even grass hoppers.

[2]This idea is reflected in Rupert Sheldrake's work with morphic
resonance, which shows that there are energetic fields that organize all
form. These fields can pass on characteristics to "unrelated" aspects of
the same species that are not necessarily in physical proximity to each
other.

[3]Highly condensed energy manifesting as light.

[4]These negative/positive orientations are not judgments. It is representative of the idea of poles, equal but possessing opposite energy.

[5]Vega is the Alpha star (the brightest) in the Lyra constellation.

4

The Sirius Factor

"Blazing as the star that cometh forth at Harvest-time,
shining forth amid the host of stars
in the darkness of the night, the star whose name
men call Orion's Dog. Brightest of all is he, yet
for an evil sign is he set, and bringeth much
fever upon hapless men..."

—The Iliad

"He comes richly dight in many colors..."

—M. Martin
(1907)

The realm of Sirius was one of the first to be explored by the curious consciousness that passed through the Prism of Lyra and fragmented from the Founders. Sirius represents a very important symbol for the entire galactic family—that of the triad. Though it has not been scientifically validated by most astronomers, Sirius is a trinary star group.[1] Symbolically, this represents the template—two polarities at the base of a triangle, and the joining or integrating of the polarities at the apex. It reflects the basic foundation of the galactic family's desire—to once again unify through the merging of polarity.

After the Infusion, many consciousnesses who chose to remain nonphysical attracted themselves to the realm of Sirius. Here they began laying the physical as well as nonphysical groundwork for the vital role Sirius was to play in the unfolding drama. They were to become some of the earliest genetic and etheric engineers following in the footsteps of the Founders.

Anticipating what was to come, these nonphysical Sirians began forming (through the transmutation of energy into matter) a third-density world that would eventually be able to support physical life. They also created more vibrationally focused realms for the consciousness that would choose to exist there in the nonphysical state. Thus, because of their ability to create realms suitable for all manifestations of consciousness, they became known as the Elders of Sirius.

During the Lyran and Vegan conflicts, representatives from both polarities inhabited the Sirius realm with the desire to integrate there. The Elders of Sirius prepared for an influx of both positive and negative energy. They were quite aware of the scenario that needed to occur.

The Vegans who chose to inhabit the Sirius realm decided to incarnate physically within a third-density reality. Culturally they were highly polarized in the masculine, and their philosophy was one of domination, which was becoming more difficult to maintain in fourth density. They felt they must dominate their environment and control their evolution. According to them, this would allow them a mastership of their realm, and from that point their evolution would then progress at an accelerated pace.

From this desire the Vegans began plans for their colonization of a planet orbiting one of the Sirius suns. If they were to maintain their philosophic orientation of domination, the natural polarization inherent in this philosophy could only be perpetuated in a third-density existence. They were to be tightly focused in the physical, creating a veil of illusion and forgetfulness even more dense than presently on Earth. They were so sure of their own abilities (and so unaware of the lure of third-density separation) that they zealously began speeding up the evolutionary process of the primate-like species developing on the world they had chosen. Soon the DNA of the indigenous species matched their desire, and they began incarnating.

Almost immediately, these new Sirians lost their memory connection with Vega. The veil was too dense. Their desire to create forgetfulness was so strong that they remembered nothing of their origin. They did not dream. They did not meditate. They did not pursue creative activities except to maintain their structure of domination. When their zealousness translated into physical reality, it created a culture driven by the desire for domination—over each other and the universe around them.

As this negative Sirian planet was developing, a group from Lyra decided to venture outward into the Sirius system. These beings chose to remain in the nonphysical realms. Their orientation was polarized toward the idea of service to others. They were particularly interested in the physical healing of those in pain. The combination of the negative Sirians (who denied their spiritual self) and the positive, nonphysical Sirians originally from Lyra (who felt it was their duty to heal all those in pain) created a dynamic of tension that echoed throughout the Sirius system and beyond.

The saga began. The positives began bombarding the negatives with love and healing energy on the subconscious and unconscious levels. Because the negatives were so tightly focused, this created psychological pain for them. The

more the negatives resisted, the more the positives sent healing energy. Friction occurred from this interaction that was
very uncomfortable for all of the consciousness in the Sirius
system. The Elders of Sirius finally intervened.

It was decided that the conflict would once again be moved
to another locale. This time integration would be attempted
from a slightly less polarized perspective. The Elders sought
out a home for this conflict. It did not take them long to
discover the electromagnetic properties of the area called
Orion. Thus the myth begins of how Sirius, the Dog Star,
leads the way for the Hunter—Orion.

Once the initial conflict was removed from the Sirius
system, the physical civilization remained. They had cut
themselves off from spirit even to the point of death, where
an immediate reincarnation into the system occurred again,
further alienating them from any form of nonphysical existence. Therefore, most of the negative society was unaware
of a conflict, so they could not be made aware of its movement
into the Orion system. Their society continued within its haze
of forgetfulness. Those desiring the negative/positive integration now went to Orion from Lyra/Vega instead of to
Sirius. Sometimes, very infrequently, a soul would awaken
from the negative Sirius world and progress to the Orion
arena.

From the positive (nonphysical) Sirius perspective, they
would now be able to directly influence the ailing negatives.
Many joyously ventured to Orion to carry out this task.
Others chose to remain within the Sirius realm, concentrating
their healing abilities toward other goals. Other positives
from Lyra joined the Orion struggle. Galactic history was
born.

Because of the positive Sirians' desire to facilitate physical
healing (their service to physicality instead of choosing incar-

nation), they allied themselves with the energies of Arcturus. Arcturus is oriented toward the idea of emotional healing. Together they form the Sirius/Arcturus Matrix. This matrix has found its way onto nearly every physical planet within the galactic family as a holistic energy representing the healing of body, mind, and spirit.

Planet Earth has known the Sirius/Arcturus Matrix in many forms. It is an archetypal energy that is used by an individual or society for many purposes. It is malleable and can be shaped into any appropriate definition. Whatever the shape, it is devoted to the service of physicality. The Sirius/Arcturus Matrix reminds the fragments of their connection to the Whole and their natural abilities for self-healing.

Though it is only a small percentage, a group of positive Sirians decided to incarnate into physicality as well. However, they rejected the humanoid form for a form that is more representative of their nature. This form is the cetacean. Dolphins and whales represent a translation of Sirius energy upon a physical, polarized world. In archetypal symbology, water represents the subconscious. Cetaceans are there silently—in Earth's oceans and in the sea of humanity's subconscious. They remain as a reminder of humanity's potential for integration.

Of all the energies that are a part of the immediate galactic family, the Sirius energy is the most widely used upon Earth. The name Sirius means "The Sparkling One" or "The Scorching One," also called the "The Dog Star" and the "The Nile Star." Perhaps because it is the brightest and the second nearest star visible to Earth (8.7 light years away), many ancient cultures recognized the importance of the Sirius energy, most notably the Egyptians.

At times, Sirius consciousness may choose to densify its frequency to become visible to third-density humans. During many of the Egyptian dynasties it was quite common to have a visitation from a Sirian in the disguise of one of their gods (such as Isis, Osiris, and Anubis). These "costumes" made it easier for the Egyptians to honor their presence, and often the visitations triggered memories of the very early days when the "gods" walked openly upon Earth. These Sirians gave the Egyptians (as well as other Earth cultures) much advanced astronomical and medical information which scholars are still questioning the origin of today.

Halfway across the globe, the Mayan culture had its own unique relationship with the Sirius. Advanced medical practices and galactic astronomical information were imparted to them that presently have not been unraveled by modern scholars. Theirs was a much more personal relationship with Sirius. These Mayans were, in a sense, tourists from the Sirius realm (incarnate here on Earth) who wanted to experience physicality from a closer vantage point. Their relationship with the Mayans was so intimate that the Sirians actually shared with them the technology of transmutation— from matter to pure energy/consciousness. When their lessons were complete, the Mayan race vanished (transmuted), leaving behind a trail for humanity to follow.

These Sirians left behind many time capsules and puzzles for future generations to discover. One of these puzzles is the crystal skull.

The crystal skull can represent the infinite nature of man and consciousness. Looking into its depths, one can sense the past and future. Humans have not yet learned how to translate the data and emotions that are triggered when one gazes into its expanse. Perhaps one day information encoded within the skull may ignite sparks of memory within humanity, as the

Sirians have possibly intended. They are one of the primary groups who, in many forms, have left the clues about Earth's past.

It is important to note that the Sirians are not meant to be spoken about as a group of extraterrestrials as much as a group consciousness that expresses itself both physically and non-physically. They have been a guiding force for the developing civilization upon Earth. As will be explored in later chapters, they are one of the primary characters in the creation of the human species on Earth.

Returning now to the negative Sirius planet, Earth has an analogous translation of its philosophy. The practice that is called "black magic" or the "dark arts" is rooted in the philosophy of the negative Sirians. Within the Egyptian culture the organized worship of the negative force took place within the temples and priesthoods of Set. This philosophy rejects the idea of reinclusion into the universal fabric. Those that practice this philosophy consider themselves unique, separate, and egocentric. The illusion that they have created is one of nonresponsibility for their actions. It often takes them many lessons and sometimes many lifetimes to recognize that their actions and their beliefs create the very reality they are trying to escape from.

In translation, another manifestation of the Sirius influence on Earth from a slightly negative perspective is the Illuminati. The Illuminati are a group of physical and nonphysical negatively oriented (and even some positively oriented) extraterrestrials who came to Earth as physical beings during the Inception.[2]

These beings eventually felt they did not get the recognition (or power) they thought they deserved.[3] Many of these early off-planet consciousnesses who interacted with humanity had allowed their energies or their "histories" to evolve and become an archetype to assist Earth. The idea of control is their identity. In their eyes, if they cannot control others, they do not exist. They are terrified of nonexistence. This motivation has caused them to attempt to interfere in Earth's development from the start. As with an annoying insect, they are a bother, but rarely cause serious problems. Only the individuals who have no sense of their own power will be found in those power structures upon Earth that stem from fear of powerlessness. They cannot be an influence if one does not allow them to be. It all comes back to the issue of claiming one's own power.

One final idea concerning contemporary manifestations of the Sirius energy has to do with the appearance of menacing extraterrestrials as seen in UFO literature. For the most part, severely negative UFO experiences, cattle mutilations, and the "Men in Black" phenomenon are connected to the negative Sirius (and Orion) group who actually generate more fear than damage. At times the physical Sirians (and Orions) can break through the layers of protection in the solar system and try to wreak havoc. What is their motivation?

In exploring the ancient Sumerian texts concerning early history and the nature of the conflicts of the gods, one gets a clear idea that Earth (in whole or in part) was involved with issues of territorial dispute by various groups at different times. The question has often been asked why the Sirians seem to be so involved in Earth's development. If it is indeed true that Sirius is a trinary star group (as the Dogon tribe's astronomical traditions suggest), could it be that Sol (Earth's sun) is or once was the third star? If that is the case, Earth may have been part of a territorial dispute among the Sirians from its very inception. This could explain why the negative Sirians consider it to be their right to do as they wish on Earth and why they point an accusing finger at other extraterrestrials for wrongly interfering with Sirian internal affairs, thus creating many historical disputes. The Sirians may consider Earth to be part of their territory. In present time, Sol is only 8.7 light years away from the Sirius system which has been considered by astronomers to be part of our local star family.

Many of the early Sirians were quite adept at genetic engineering. During the Earth Inception the physical Sirians placed a latent DNA code within the early humans. When Earth beings reach a certain vibratory frequency as a race, this code will be triggered. This code will assist those on Earth in remembering humanity's galactic past. Contemporary negative Sirians are terrified of this. They have continually kept themselves from transitioning into fourth density for fear of nonexistence. They fear that if *Earth* transitions, *they* will transition also and cease to exist. They believe if they keep society in fear, Earth will not be able to make the shift. As a whole, they cannot determine humanity's fate, for Earth humans have more power than the negative Sirians realize. But they will continue. They know no other way.

Whether dealing with physical extraterrestrials or archetypal energy, the Sirian identity is entwined with humanity's. It is rich with knowledge as well as challenge. One must always remember Sirius as the triad and what it represents—integration from polarity—which is the destiny of Earth.

---

[1] Some astronomers, such as Van Den Bos and Finsen at the Union Observatory in the 1920s, and more recently, D. Lauterborn, are theorizing that Sirius is indeed a trinary star group, but no viable data has been uncovered to confirm that claim.

[2] The Illuminati are not only comprised of Sirians. Other groups, such as Orion, are part of the Illuminati structure.

[3] These beings represent only a small percentage of Sirius consciousness. Since the Earth Inception, the planet has developed some very strong positive relationships with Sirius beings who have been some of the main supporters of humanity from the beginning.

5

The Winds of Orion

"Begirt with many a blazing star,
Stood the great giant Algebar,
Orion, hunter of the beast!
His sword hung gleaming by his side,
And on his arm, the lion's hide
Scattered across the midnight air
The Golden radiance of its hair..."

—Longfellow

"Canst thou bind the sweet influence of the Pleiades,
or loose the bands of Orion?"

—Job 38:31

When two opposite polarities meet, they are naturally attracted. When they attempt fusion (rather than integration) they produce a force of enormous energy. They produce sparks. They produce change. Sometimes they even produce pain.

This was the case with the civilizations of Lyra that attempted integration within the Sirius star system. The conflict began playing out within Sirius, but was energetically moved to Orion. Its beginnings were as a Lyran conflict. Through generations it evolved into a new races' war, that of the Orions. As generations passed, each side lost touch with what they were fighting for. Yet the anguish continued.

The stakes were clearly marked. The "negative" side perpetuated the idea of service to self. Within their philosophy, if one served the self the whole was served. What they did not realize was that they were *denying* the whole by the way they chose to carry out this philosophy. This translated as the need for domination.

These were dark times indeed. Domination entailed behavior that Earth humans have never experienced. Genetic manipulation of blood lines was common, in an attempt to dilute or concentrate power. What humans know as black magic was a common practice. Beings were so saturated with their own fear that they struck out at all who were different. The Earth legends of sword and sorcery are dim remembrances carried in the etheric cell memory from the dark times of Orion.

The "positive" side epitomized the idea of service to others. It was their belief that the only way to survive was to be subservient, even at the expense of the self. So an interesting dynamic was played out. There were those individuals who were the dominators and those who were all to willing to play the victim role. These "positives" felt that to support the whole they must serve the whole and relinquish the self. In reality they were denying themselves as being a valid portion of that whole.

The Orion civilization was one of the very few that evolved into a state of technological advancement while still being spiritually depraved. Eons of time passed while the drama continued playing out. It began with basic emotional manipulation all the way to the other end of the spectrum—manipulation using highly advanced technological tools. Reincarnationally speaking, the same souls incarnated time and again, switching sides, trying to find a way to bring the whole struggle into balance.

Within Orion history there has always been underground resistance. Throughout the ages its strength ebbed and flowed like the pulses of their red giant Betelgeuse. Usually they would be discovered by the "negatives," disbanded, and punished. Anytime they built up some momentum, it radiated too loudly and they were found.

As the philosophy of the resistance solidified, it became apparent that they needed to squelch the radiation of their ideas. They decided instead to symbolically absorb. They allowed people to come to *them*. They became like a black hole—unable to be seen, but the force and momentum of their energy was as powerful as a silent wind. Their organization was thus called "The Black League." The symbol of their struggle became the black dragon. A new aspect of the drama began to unfold.

Now there were three facets to the struggle: There were the dominators, the victims, and the resistance (fueled by the friction of two polarities). The Black League became quite successful in thwarting the efforts of the dominators; however, it was only enough to reduce their momentum to a standstill. An energy impasse was reached.

Within the souls of these repressed people existed a great desperation. They knew the extent of the Orion Empire's control. The Empire had devised ways to control astral bodies; death was no longer freedom. Many individuals studied with heretic teachers to learn the ancient knowledge of dimensional consciousness travel. Few were successful, but those who were found a way out of the Orion system forever. Through focused concentration and disengagement from the Orion mass-conscious belief systems, a small percentage of individuals were able to leave their bodies (die) and successfully target or home in on beings who had escaped or were reincarnated on Earth from Orion.[1] Once these beings were targeted, the Orion entity was able to create a window through which he/she could travel. When he/she came through that window and incarnated on Earth, that being became "lost" in the Earth mass consciousness. This was a safety mechanism; if they did not know their identity, they could not be pursued by the Orion Empire.

The escapees would then enter Earth's reincarnational cycle and most likely continue to play out the Orion drama unconsciously within their soul patterns. At times they are immediately pursued through the window by Orion Empire representatives. Often these Empire representatives become "caught" in Earth's mass consciousness as well and must enter the reincarnational cycle; when they incarnate they carry their old Orion desire for control with them.

As the desperation grew, the Black League decided to fight even harder. They had people who played both sides of the fence. Smuggled reports from informants resulted in an even more intense resistance effort. They began to employ tactics borrowed from the dominators. All this was done in the name of freedom. As they quickly learned, freedom was elusive, and the conflict intensified.

With all of their efforts the Black League could not understand why they were not being successful in liberating the victims. They became discouraged. The people hungered for a form of spirituality, but all that was present was a gnawing emptiness and fear. Nothing worked. For a few generations, the Black League remained stagnant, only an idea and nothing more.

Then something miraculous occurred. During generations of gestation a seed began to grow. A soul incarnated who embodied all the hopes and dreams of the Orion races and with none of the hatred or fear. When he was born, he was safely contained in an energetically and emotionally neutral environment deep within the planet so he would not become polarized. At adulthood he began to teach. What he taught began to shed new light on the struggle. What he proposed could end it once and for all.

He taught universal laws—positivity cannot be achieved through negativity. The Black League was fighting fire with fire, only creating a blaze instead of peace. One must integrate positivity and negativity to the balance point. One must *love*, not fear. The idea of peace and freedom must be loved so much that one is willing to *live* it in one's soul despite outside manifestations. The Black League thus learned that their intentions were good, but their actions only caused more of what they despised.

This realization occurred on mass levels. It opened new doors of spirituality for the people of these oppressed worlds. They had a long way to go, but at least they now knew where to start.

Once the dynamic began to be understood from higher levels, it was decided that they would transmute this energy by moving outward into the galaxy and starting fresh. From these higher levels they called upon the Founders to assist them in choosing a world. Of primary concern was an assurance that all the tools were provided on this new world for these adventurous beings to begin transmutation of the Orion energy. Free Will/Choice was the primary tool, as well as a latent DNA code that would trigger a desire for societal preservation when/if it became possible for them to self-destruct. The world that was chosen was Earth. The

Founders then began engaging various physical groups to carry out the Earth Inception.

Earth has manifested the Orion drama in an attempt to balance polarity throughout humankind's history. The fall of Atlantis, the Roman Empire, and the ongoing religious wars are all examples of memory patterns from Orion that are emerging to be cleared. Throughout all of these dramas the human race has survived and has kept total oppression at bay. Humanity continues to play out the same dynamic: victims, perpetrators, and resistance. However, this time light is beginning to spread and even the resistance is beginning to learn early on that one can't fight fire with fire.

The contemporary Orion civilization, existing in the same time continuum as present-day Earth, has already healed its conflict. Because Earth is still playing out Orion's *past* in an attempt to balance it for itself, the primary contact humanity receives from Orion has been judged to be negative. The Men in Black phenomenon as well as some manifestations of the Illuminati structure are playing out the past Orion need for control.

The Men in Black (MIBs) have several origins. Some are human incarnations from Orion and/or negatively oriented Sirius energy; others are actual past Orions who have traveled "forward" in time to present-day Earth. (These include Empire representatives who were caught in Earth's mass consciousness as they pursued Orion escapees.) They perceive Earth as a threat. From their point of view, as humanity awakens and liberates itself it magnetizes the oppressed Orion beings to seek freedom here. They want to keep these windows of opportunity closed for the victims of Orion, keep Earth unempowered, and stay in total control. The MIBs are only one manifestation of this idea; generally it is played out on Earth in a much more subtle way. Those individuals who carry the oppressive patterns from Orion act from their soul memory and are not necessarily conscious in their desire for absolute control. In researching twentieth-century MIB en-counters, one comes across the ironic behavior of these beings—they function at a very autonomous level and seem to never claim for themselves the power that they so single-mindedly attempt to wrest from humans. This may suggest that the MIB is only a pawn in a perhaps an even more bizarre power struggle.

The Orion drama is not an experiment done *to* someone *by* someone else. All those who choose to be a part of the Earth Transmutation do so through their Free Will. This Transmutation/Integration will affect the entire galactic fami-ly that was created through the Dimensional Infusion. This would initiate the beginning processes of the Integration back through the Prism of Lyra. The integrated polarities can thus be termed the "Orion Light."

There were stages built into the Transmutation project from which the founders would be able to gauge its progress. The first stage was a simple seeding and developing of third-density life into a strong genetic strain on Earth. The subsequent stages involved various developments of civiliza-tion. The crucial stage is occurring presently upon the Earth—the mass reawakening of millions of souls to a greater spiritual purpose.

This awakening occurs naturally and begins to accelerate a widening of the gap between the positive and negative poles (as seen presently within society). The accentuation of this gap serves to polarize and highlight the choices society may take—making it clear that choices *must* be made at this point in time. Humanity does not have the ugliness and pain of a tormented past to the extent that the Orions had. As Earth reawakens, all the tools become visible for humanity to claim responsibility for the Whole and the Self. The painful Orion memories may continue to surface, but the healing of them will occur through humanity's proclamation of freedom and choice.

When the Dimensional Infusion occurred, there were some individual and group consciousnesses who chose to remain dormant. They allowed themselves to serve as archetypes, and could be awakened as needed. Some even allowed fragments of themselves to incarnate. An example of this is the consciousness known as Merlin. During the time of the Orion drama the friction between the two polarities awakened the sleeping magician. "He" became a guiding force in the drive to integrate from both a physical and a nonphysical point of view. Fragments of his consciousness would incarnate intermittently to spark a memory of the past and a vision of the future. He has gone by many names on many worlds, but he always mirrors one's own beauty as well as one's ugliness. His energy has been present in association with Earth right from the Inception.

The Earth Inception will be examined more thoroughly in the coming chapters. For the time being, it must be shared that this drama has been created to be a success. Most who incarnate upon Earth are involved (to varying degrees) in the Orion drama. Everyone is here by choice. The instant that one begins operating from a belief that humanity is here against its will is the instant that personal and planetary power has been surrendered.

---

[1]The Orions had the capability to target Earth individuals in Earth's past, present and future.

6

Earth's Pleiadian Cousins

"Many a night from yonder ivied casement
ere I went to rest,
Did I look upon great Orion,
sloping slowly to the west.
Many a night I saw the Pleiads,
rising thro' the mellow shade
Glitter like a swarm of fireflies
tangled in a silver braid."

—Tennyson

During the early development of the Lyran system the first friction between polarities began to occur. Some Lyrans manifested the idea of the feminine polarity—intuitive and allowing. They believed the path to reintegration was through inner development. Other Lyrans, however, polarized to the masculine. Their philosophy upheld the notion that in order to evolve, they had to dominate the known universe. This caused much dissension between the two.

As the Lyran civilization developed, a group of Lyrans decided they would prefer to develop their culture away from what they perceived were negative influences. Thus they searched the galaxy for a new home. In their search they found a young planet rich in natural resources. This planet was Earth.

For several generations this group resided on Earth, coexisting peacefully with the developing primate race. However, over a long period of time they found that they were not adapting to Earth's physical and electromagnetic environment as well as they desired. During this time they incorporated small amounts of genetic material from the primates to assist them in assimilating to Earth's environment. Over generations their DNA changed slightly, allowing them to become more adapted to Earth.

While these Earth-Lyrans were incorporating primate genetics into themselves, other groups of Lyrans were on the planet to carry out the Founders' wishes as well as their own by inserting Lyran genetics into the primates. The arrival of these Lyrans refueled the conflicts the Earth-Lyrans initially escaped from, so they chose to find another planetary system to colonize. Desiring to build a new culture where they could become isolated from old conflicts rooted in their past, they explored the region widely before they decided on an open cluster of young blue stars known as the Pleiades.[1]

When the Pleiadian star system began to be colonized by Earth-Lyrans it was intended to be a very balanced, independent race. This was reflected in their choice of a new, stable star cluster. More than anything else, they desired to create a culture based on harmony, truth, and unconditional love. Once the colonization plan became known, others of Lyran descent who felt they had no intense drama to play out decided to colonize other areas of the Pleiades star cluster.

These early Pleiadians (the previous Earth-Lyrans) possessed highly developed intuitive skills, as well as an inbred desire to create a community lifestyle. The Whole was as important as the Self. Even with this desire, it took these beings centuries to mature and create their own identity separate from their Lyran roots. For generations they developed this new culture which was philosophical in nature and technologically progressing at a rate perfect for their development. Though there were several periods of conflict, the cultural base that these new Pleiadians created remained stable for many thousands of years.

Over centuries the community-oriented Pleiadians began to favor peace and tranquility so much that they learned to invalidate all forms of negativity. Deeper and deeper they submerged their natural humanoid tendencies, until a great emptiness appeared within their being. There was no conflict, resolution, or learning. A voice cried out from within them. There was a portion of them that desired to be heard.

From this well of despair they reached out to their Lyran forefathers. When the call was answered, the Lyrans were surprised to find a culture that had virtually cut itself off from creation. The Pleiadians had no knowledge of what was occurring in the universe around them. They were unaware of the anguish of Orion, even though they too were descendants of Lyra.

When the Pleiadians were made aware of the Orion struggle, their own sleeping dragon awakened. They felt a passion. Once again they felt alive; a deep mission was sparked within their souls. They offered to be of service within the Orion struggle. It was then that they committed themselves to fighting the Orion negativity.

Thus it began. They entered the Orion struggle through many vehicles. Some souls chose to incarnate directly into the system within both polarity orientations (positive and negative) in order to understand the struggle. The majority of these Pleiadians incarnating into the Orion struggle became ensnared—it is easy to enter the Orion reincarnational cycle but virtually impossible to escape. Others chose to ally themselves with the Black League or continue to incarnate within the Pleiadian system and attempt to contain the expansion of the Orion Empire. They fought with every ounce of their being against the negativity they saw around them. Unconsciously they also fought the negativity still further—within themselves.

The struggle continued. The Pleiadians fought as zealously against the Orion negativity as they did their own latent shadow selves. Instead of finding a truth within, they only perpetuated their hatred of their own negativity. It was only when the Orion Empire destroyed one of their populated planets that they disengaged themselves actively from the Orion struggle. The lifeless, charred planet still stands in their system as a reminder of their past actions. When that planet was obliterated, the Pleiadians were devastated. Finally, an impasse was reached.

On the highest levels of being, every consciousness involved in the Orion drama took a step back. They evaluated the situation. It became obvious that the resolution needed to occur from a different angle. They agreed to extend the conflict to another arena within the galaxy. The Pleiadians were faced with a choice: would they return their energies to their home worlds, or would they agree to resolve their own issues (as well as the Orion struggle) once and for all?

Initially, they chose to return home. This allowed them to gather their strength and search the very depths of their souls to find a way to become whole. They were so afraid of the negativity that they became immobilized. They waited. They pondered...and they faltered.

While they waited, the Inception project began in full force upon the Earth. The Lyrans were the physical directors of the project (under the Founders), accepting assistance from other physical groups such as Sirius. It quickly became apparent that they needed a genetic structure of terrestrial as well as extraterrestrial origin for their Inception project. They contacted the Pleiadians.

At first the Pleiadians expressed reluctance about becoming involved with Earth once again. However, the Lyrans pointed out possible Pleiadian benefits with a deft craftiness. Knowing that the Pleiadians had originally incorporated Earth primate genetics into themselves, the Lyrans admitted that they needed certain aspects of Pleiadian DNA for the developing terran species on Earth. Unknowingly, they also created a way for the Pleiadians to face their negativity once and for all.

It was proposed that a DNA transfer from the Pleiadians into the terran species over a long period of time would create a race of humanoids who would be terrestrial but would also have extraterrestrial roots. The closest ancestors of these Earth humans would be the Pleiadians, and through these family ties the Pleiadians would be allowed to be involved with the Earth species development. During this involvement they would observe the developing race, interact intermittently in order to keep them on course, and learn about human negativity. This vicariously would heal the pain of the Pleiadian past. After some reluctance to associate once again with the Lyrans, a group of Pleiadians finally agreed.

From this agreement came thousands of years of Pleiadian interaction with nearly every primitive culture upon the Earth. Drawings of space beings and spacecraft adorn many cave walls, and many ancient documents record the actions of these gods who came from the sky. They saw themselves as "gods" no more than today's humans do. However, from the point of view of a primitive people, they surely must have seemed like gods.

During certain developmental stages of a humanoid species, it is common to give up personal power to a godlike or magical figure. This became widespread, and soon the Pleiadians began to relish the power they were given. They began to wield it. Some began using fear in order to manipulate. Their soul-level agreement to learn from the developing Earth transformed into a satiation of personal desire. Many ancient myths concerning jealous gods are directly linked to these extraterrestrial beings from other systems, including the Pleiades.[2]

When these power binges occurred, it was necessary for these extraterrestrials to be reminded of their purpose. Very often resentment built up on the part of the Pleiadians toward other visiting groups. For a period of a few thousand years the Pleiadians grew in power, and then were consistently reminded of their place. The irony of the situation soon became known to them—they had wished to get in touch with their negativity. Their wish had been granted.

During these interactions the Pleiadians involved with Earth were all from the same time continuum. Their contacts were consistent with their development. They had not yet mastered the complex technology of time/space manipulation. It wasn't until the twentieth century that Earth has begun to pull in Pleiadian contact from many different time frames simultaneously.

Though contact continued intermittently until the present day, it has slowed in comparison to earlier times. They no longer consider Earth humans to be children, and they allow humanity to make its own choices. Once Earth began its technological era, it was watched very closely for the critical mass necessary to activate the DNA code for preservation of the species. Since the 1940s both physical and nonphysical extraterrestrials have been monitoring humanity and attempting communication, mostly in subtle ways. The Pleiadians were the first to begin a major benevolent contact program physically with Earth. Although this was quietly carried out as early as the 1930s, it began to be noticed on a wider scale in the 1970s.[3]

A Swiss named Billy Meier has documented hundreds of hours of communication with the Pleiadian cosmonaut Semjase. He also possesses a large number of photographs of the Pleiadians' spacecrafts which, using photographic technology, have never been proven to be false. He claims to have been taken both backward and forward in time by the Pleiadians (and their allies the DALs) to view various events.

This contact has caused major controversy since it was revealed. Meier has been provided with evidence such as a metal sample which was analyzed on film by a noted IBM scientist. The metal sample subsequently disappeared, but the film analysis remains. Within the UFO research community this case is a classic example of throwing the baby out with the bathwater. Because it is "too easy," it is considered a hoax. When Meier attempted to construct models of Pleiadian spacecrafts to see if the photographs could be faked, the models were found, and the whole case was labeled a hoax.

The teachings of the 1970s from Semjase and her associates are now beginning to be more widely known. They teach spiritual truths as well as give a partial history of the Pleiadian race. Some teachings warn of impending natural and man-made disasters connected with a new age to come. It seems that these Pleiadian beings are from a time/space in their history where this method of communication represented their primary philosophy. Though these teachings may have been applicable when they were given, one may question how they relate to today's mass consciousness.

There are indications that the mass consciousness of Earth made a shift from a future of disaster to one of increasing responsibility during the time period of 1980–1982. Since these Pleiadian teachings originated before the shift was made, perhaps they represent an old idea. It does not necessarily mean they are not valid, but it does mean that perhaps there is a different outlook coming to humanity instead—one which reflects the choices and changes humanity has recently made on a mass-conscious level.

The Pleiadian contact coming to us presently (both in physical and telepathic forms) may echo a different voice. Some claim to be the future descendants of Meier's Pleiadians. These Pleiadians speak openly of their difficult past and why they felt they needed to use certain tactics in dealing with Earth. They admit to having their own motivations for contact, and thank this planet for all they have learned. They are helping society to shed light on other forms of contact that they themselves are not directly involved in (such as negative abduction experiences). They are sincerely assisting humanity by whatever means they can, allowing the planet to achieve a global as well as galactic viewpoint.

The Pleiadians have specific reasons for being tentative in their present interactions with Earth. For thousands of years they have stepped in either to protect us from danger or to control us like children "for our own good." Some splinter groups even manipulated humankind for its own purposes. This has been a source of great shame to them. They now realize that humanity must make *its own* choices and they must trust Earth's ability to do so. They have created a karmic cycle through their interference. For their own growth, it is imperative that this cycle be relinquished. The thought of perpetuating the pattern of interference on Earth is the single most fearful idea facing a Pleiadian.

Will Pleiadian contact with Earth continue in the future? Since they are the most similar to the Earth human physically (in fourth-density form), it seems appropriate that they become one of the first to walk this planet undisguised. They stress, however, that as much as humanity might want to meet its cousins from the sky, they will not initiate an open contact program until humanity can embrace its brothers across the street. It is up to this planet. It is *humanity* who is calling the shots. Are we finally ready to let go of the fear of recognizing our heritage and accept their outstretched hands?

---

1 Splinter groups also colonized other systems in Earth's galactic neighborhood.

2 Examples of these myths include the Egyptian accounts of Set and Osiris, as well as the Sumerian conflicts between Enlil and Enki. These seem like archetypal battles; many cultures have legends of similar figures that can be considered counterparts, or perhaps a translation of one story.

3 There are indications that negative groups (such as the Sirians) began contact in the 1930s as well and that their negative actions were always countered by the more benevolent groups such as the Pleiadians. This heavy contact activity (by both positively and negatively oriented groups) appears to occur in 20-year cycles: 1930s, 1950s, 1970s, and as we will soon perhaps see, the 1990s.

7

The Gateway of Arcturus

"Verily, when a person departs from this world
he goes to the wind.
It opens out there for him like
the hole of a chariot wheel.
Through it he mounts higher.
He goes to the sun.
It opens out there for him like the hole of a drum...
He goes to the moon...
He goes to the world that is without sorrow..."

—Brihad-Aranyaka Upanishad

When passing through the Prism of Lyra, there were some beings who decided to remain in nonphysical form. These beings lovingly chose an existence of service to those of the more dense realities, such as third-density Earth. They realized that on developing physical worlds the evolving life may need assistance from other realms. This assistance would come in the form of archetypes, angels, guides, and unseen inspiration.

These beings were attracted to the area of the star Arcturus. During their initial attraction the star field in the Arcturus region was slightly different from its present manifestation, but the energy of the area remains constant. There is a gateway or crossroad in the fabric of time and space in the general area of Arcturus. These beings soon realized that this gateway passes dimensionally through almost every other area that became inhabited from the Dimensional Infusion. It was then that they began to understand their purpose—to aid consciousness from many levels of awareness.

The Arcturan purpose is multifaceted. One idea is that they serve humanoidkind as an ideal. They represent the future self of an individual or a society. Their energy is, by its nature, a magnet that draws out positivity from the very depths of being. They reflect to Earth where it is heading in its evolution. Once humanity evolves into nonphysicality, the ideal goal is to achieve a consciousness similar to that of the Arcturan mass consciousness. They recognize themselves as a group matrix, committed to the idea of the evolution of consciousness.

Very often Arcturan beings will manifest to humans as angels. It is known that one of the purposes of an angel is to serve humankind. In a very real sense, the Arcturans have a dedication to humanoidkind. They have chosen to learn about physicality through physical beings.

They are etheric in nature. Their energy can be felt as a presence, a surge of creativity or unconditional love. They will manifest according to the belief system of the person they are interacting with. To the more traditionally religious, it will be as angels. To some of the more modern seekers, perhaps as extraterrestrials or future selves. Either way the outcome is the same—an interaction with a truly loving, selfless being devoted to the service of physical beings and thus the Whole.

Because they serve physicality they interact not only with the humanoid beings upon a planet, but also with the unseen kingdoms whose evolution is different from that of humanoids. Each planet has its own devic kingdom—the consciousness energy of the plant, mineral, and animal kingdoms—and the Arcturan energy acts as a higher aspect of a planet's devic kingdom. Again, they repeat the idea of reflecting the future evolutionary ideal.

There are a small number of Arcturans who choose to experience physicality in order to serve. Rather than entering physicality through the birth process, they choose to "walk in" an already existing body on a physical world. They do not have the need (or the "karmic compulsion," so to speak) to enter through the incarnation process. By various agreements between souls, a "trade" is established. The soul of a human who is emotionally in pain will enter the Arcturus realm for healing, and the curious Arcturan will temporarily embody upon a planet.[1]

The primary service that the Arcturans provide for physical beings is that of emotional healing. Arcturus is more of a realm than a place, and within the realm of Arcturus Earth souls who have had traumatic deaths (or lives) are healed and rejuvenated. Because the gateway of Arcturus connects dimensionally with Earth, *all* who incarnate on Earth must pass through the Arcturus realm before they reach the planet, unless they consciously choose not to. This provides a healing for those about to be born, and a strengthening of their choices and desires for the physical life about to occur.

The gateway of Arcturus prepares nonphysical consciousness for the intense focus of physicality and thus sexuality. From the Arcturan point of awareness, physicality and sexuality are the same expression. The Arcturus energy is particularly adept at various forms of sexual healing, such as in the case of sexual abuse during childhood or adulthood. The healing energies of Arcturus are equally nurturing for the abused and the abuser, for both are in much pain. The utilization of the Sirius/Arcturus healing matrix can be quite powerful in such cases.

The cetaceans, especially dolphins, can represent the Sirius/Arcturus matrix to those in pain. Since dolphins are quite sexual and unconditionally loving in their expression, they can serve as a physical manifestation of the Sirius/Arcturus healing matrix. This matrix is totally non-threatening, providing subtle healing on very deep levels.

At death the human consciousness passes through the Arcturus realm. There they are nurtured and cared for until they awaken to their greater reality. In the case of traumatic death, a great tenderness and healing is shared in order that the soul about to awaken makes a smooth transition.

In after-death experiences the light that is perceived at the end of a tunnel is actually a representation of the Arcturus vibration. This vibration will be translated through the perceiver's own belief system. Because Arcturus is primarily sixth density, it is often perceived as the Christ or Buddha vibration. The light can be equated with the future or higher self (Christ self) of an individual. So in a sense, during the death process one is merging with the higher self, which happens to share a frequency range nearly identical to the Arcturus realm. There healing occurs. In all of creation there is nothing that heals, nurtures, and rejuvenates the human spirit as completely as Arcturus.[2]

Another idea that is synonymous with the Arcturus vibration is the idea of creativity. When one is creating, one aligns with the energy of the Creator. Since Arcturus serves as a "messenger" of the Creator, so to speak, the vibrations are quite similar. In this way Arcturus has been intimately bound to humanity from the beginning, since humanity is always creating.

Arcturus is much more than a star. It is a frequency that one possesses within. It is a frequency of creation, healing, and evolution. It has been with Earth and other developing physical planets from their inception. It is less a character in the galactic family story than an undercurrent—one that is ever present in the entire Dimensional Infusion idea.

Because the energy of Arcturus is an undercurrent that consistently interacts with us, the Earth planetary environment often translates Arcturan energy into a form that is meant to trigger individuals emotionally. An example of this is the lenticular cloud, a spectacular cloud formation that molds itself into a disk shape. It may look like a spacecraft, but most of the time it is merely the Earth environment translating the energy it perceives at an etheric level. These etheric "ships" serve once again to remind humanity of its unseen connections.

Within polarized reality Arcturus has chosen a counterpart to reflect other aspects of its evolving nature. Its counterpart is the area called Antares. Within the dimensional gateway or crossroad there is a joining between Antares and Arcturus that serves as a major focal point of energy in this region. Most of the consciousnesses who incarnate on Earth pass only through the Arcturus vibration. There are others who choose to pass through Antares before they reach Arcturus. These are the individuals who work directly with mass-consciousness patterns, matrices, and cellular evolution.

Antares is also the dimensional connection point between Earth's quadrant of the Milky Way and the galaxy called Andromeda. The Antares/Andromeda connection energizes the abstract concepts of existence and consciousness necessary for physical races to begin to remember their heritage, thus transmuting their past.

Most of the other races explored in this work have more individualized agreements with planet Earth. The Arcturus connection is very fluid, very malleable, but no less important. If one likens all the other characters of the story to ingredients in a cosmic soup, one can see how they all add to the flavoring. However, if one likens Arcturus to the consistency of the bouillon in the soup, it is apparent how the Arcturan vibration is a vital ingredient that holds it all together.

Many manifestations of the Arcturan energy on Earth can be explored. First, one can say that Arcturus and Sirius form a partnership. Whereas Arcturus works with emotional healing, Sirius facilitates physical healing. The Egyptians knew these connections and called upon the energies of the Arcturus/Sirius matrix for assistance in their rituals. The Egyptian deity known as Anubis was a direct Sirian archetype, but worked with the Arcturan energy. Anubis guided individuals into the underworld (the astral), or through the process of physical death. There the energies of both Sirius and Arcturus began the healing process with the soul. The representation of the jackal (or the "dog," as in the Dog Star of Sirius) as Anubis is a blatant signal that the Egyptians were aware of the connection. Anubis (as a Sirius archetype) leads the departed soul to the Arcturus realm where healing occurs.

Arcturus represents the positivity within humanity as much as Orion represents the negative or conflicting nature. The archetype of Merlin has often been labeled a bridge. When two polarities attempt a unification, there must be a common ground they both stand on before the merging occurs. Merlin is thus a bridge between the explosive Orion and the healing Arcturus. He is the common ground. It is apparent how his energy has been of major importance, not only to Earth, but to all who experience polarity. Magic is the spark created from the friction between polarities that ignites transformation.

Early in the development of the Earth, the Arcturans agreed to densify themselves enough to be perceived temporarily. They interacted with the early culture that was Lemuria by teaching healing skills. The memory of these interactions was carried throughout generations. When the Lemurians migrated to many areas of Earth, these memories were carried with them. The statues of Easter Island are one of the few ideas that remain in the physical of their direct interaction. These statues are not meant to represent these densified Arcturans so much as to pay them tribute. Their position is skyward, gazing at the horizon, waiting for their return.

Humanity has never had to wait for their return. The energy has been present all along. If one looks inward instead of outward, they can be found. They are the human race evolved to its highest potential. They remind humanity and edge it forward into the magnificent spiral of evolution. Home is where the heart is, and the heart is the path of Arcturus.

---

[1]It needs to be clarified here that this is not a common occurrence. Many who claim to be "walk ins" have experienced a more common process that can be called "soul-braiding." This process is the bringing in of a higher frequency of the soul's *own* energy, *not* an exchange of consciousness. It can be mistakenly understood as the entrance of a new consciousness, whereas it is a stepping up and integration of the original consciousness.

[2]In many after-death experiences individuals have spoken poignantly of the bright light that they encounter. One such account, chronicled in Moody's *Life After Life* states, "A brilliant white light appeared to me. The light was so bright that I could not see through it, but going into its

presence was so calming and wonderful. There is just no experience on earth like it." Entering the Arcturan vibration after death can be equated with this experience.

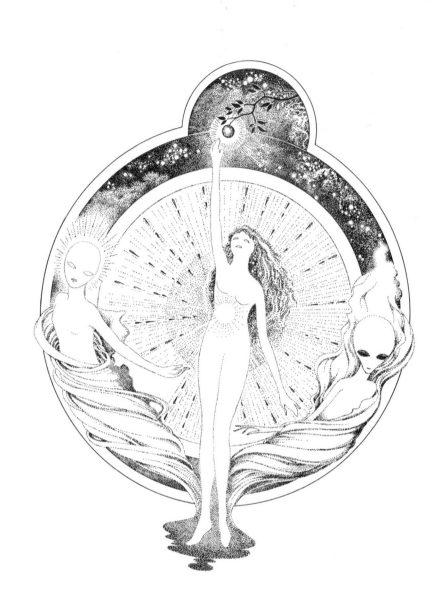

8

Earth Inception

*"Then God said, 'Let us make man
in our image, in our likeness...'"*

—Genesis
1:26

In whose image were Earth humans made? Many of Earth's oldest scriptures imply that human development was guided by gods who descended from the sky. Even anthropologists are aware of the unusually fast development of Homo sapiens. Some anthropologists estimate that the species Homo sapiens appears to be millions of years ahead of schedule.

Whereas the evolutionary development between Advanced Australopithecus and Neanderthal took more than two million years, evidence has been found on Earth that Homo sapiens (Cro-Magnon) emerged approximately 35,000 years ago. What is even more intriguing is that while the remains of man are continually discovered, archaeologists have found remains from an even *earlier* Homo sapiens in the areas of western Asia and Northern Africa. These remains date back 250,000 years *before* Cro-Magnon man. It should be stated here that Homo sapiens has no evolutionary precursor. Nothing evolved *into* Homo sapiens—the species simply *appears*.

Would extraterrestrials be interested in having a hand in Earth's evolution? If so, what could they gain from Earth humans? Perhaps it was a way for them to accelerate their *own* evolution.

It seems evident that there were three main groups that orchestrated the Earth Inception: the Founders, a Lyran group, and a Sirian group. The Founders facilitated the Inception from a point of nonphysicality and were the overseers of the entire project. Unaware of these nonphysical influences, the Lyrans physically orchestrated the Inception and employed a Sirian group to assist. Each group had its own motivations for their involvement. Though the motivations were different, the goal was the same—the creation of a humanoid race on Earth.

As stated earlier, the Pleiadians involved themselves in Earth's evolution for their own benefit. They felt that if they interacted with humans, not only would they be able to be a part of the development of their original home, but they could learn about negativity and integration without having to incarnate directly into a world that was playing those ideas out. They were persuaded by the Lyran group, who were well aware of the genetic compatibility of the Pleiadians with the new Earth humans being developed.

The Lyran group (a joint effort from various Lyran races) was always experimenting. Just as humans have certain instinctive drives (such as procreation), these extraterrestrials carry their own drives which emulate *their* "creators"—the Founders. The Founders' "offspring" instinctively carried on with genetic seeding. These Founders were well aware that inbreeding would cause a race to die out, and thus they continually sought new stock to keep the gene pool mixed.

There was another primary Lyran motivation for their involvement with Earth. After eons of conflict within the Lyran offshoot races (Vega, Sirius, Orion, etc.), they were tired of creating civilizations that were polarized and failed to exist peacefully. They were determined that Earth was to be a planet founded on integration rather than polarity. The Lyran group felt that perhaps what they needed all along was a planet whose *beginnings* were integrated rather than one that was carrying the seeds of polarity from other star systems. With this in mind they began formulating their rigid plan for the Earth Inception.

The Founders, however, had other plans. They knew that Earth was possibly going to be the final ground for healing the Orion drama, and therefore *must remain polarized* in order to resolve the conflict. The Founders knew that the galactic family might finally learn about integration through the experience of polarity resolution on Earth. The Founders allowed the Lyran group to carry out *their* plan because they knew it would eventually support the *cosmic* plan.

As for the Sirian group, their motivations were much closer to home. They considered Earth to be within the Sirius trinary star system; thus they believed they had a right to manipulate Earth genetics. The Sirians were interested in simply in establishing primitive humanoid races on Earth that could serve as manual laborers while they expanded their colonies to include Earth. Thus they supported the Lyran project with their own goals in mind. The Earth Inception project began.

For many thousands of years during the early phases of the Earth Inception project, the Lyrans[1] watched the developing primate race on earth with cautious eyes. Occasionally they took samples and made slight alterations to the DNA structures. At critical points in development they began inserting genetic material from the Pleiadians[2] (and other groups) into these primates. Over long periods it became increasingly apparent that evolution was accelerating at a rapid pace. When this became evident, the crucial prototype experiments were initiated.

The story of Adam and Eve is one of the few legacies left that can subtly remind humanity of its beginnings. The tale contains many symbolic references to the saga that occurred concerning the type of species who were to inherit the Earth.

As stated, the Lyran group wanted a species founded on integration. Therefore, they felt that the species must have no knowledge of polarity—or "good" and "evil." They strictly controlled the environment of these new humans in order that they would stay focused on developing as perfect vehicles of integration. They did not want the new humans to *become like them*—polarized. What the Lyran group did not acknowledge was that they were also restricting *choice* on the part of these new humans.

After generations of working with primates and extraterrestrial genetics, the Lyran group developed a human prototype whose meaning, "of the earth," has been translated into the name "Adam." The Adam prototype was introduced on Earth to test its environmental adaptability in many areas of the planet. (There were many Adams). When this prototype was satisfactorily adapted, the Adams were recalled.

"So the Lord God caused a deep sleep to fall upon the man, and he slept. Then He took one of his ribs [or part of his side], and closed up the flesh at that place."[3] Through cloning and genetic engineering, a female prototype was created that is translated as "Eve." Both were returned to the environment and watched closely.

Out of their desire to create a species that had no knowledge of polarity, the Lyrans instructed all who tended the prototypes to forbid them knowledge—to actually deny them the right of choice which all divine beings are granted. Hence, one can see the meaning of the statement by God: "From any tree of the garden you may eat freely; but from the tree of the knowledge of good and evil [polarity] you shall not eat, for in the day that you eat from it you shall surely die."[4]

The Sirians working with the Lyran group disagreed with this philosophy. They felt the Lyrans' personal desires for creating this species was misaligned with the rights of humanoid forms. These Sirians, although wanting to develop the human race for their own purposes, discovered they had a genuine affection for the new humans. Despite this duality they decided to intervene, thus inadvertently giving humans the opportunity to choose.

The Sirian group warned the humans. "And the serpent[5] said to the woman, 'You surely shall *not* die! For God knows that in the day you eat from it your eyes will be opened, and you will be like God, knowing good and evil.'"[6] Being presented with choice and the need for a decision involving their existence, the humans achieved third-density consciousness. When the humans realized they had been deceived by "God" they opted for knowledge. *Once they made the choice to receive knowledge of polarity they were fully anchored in the physical.* They now possessed ego, or knowledge of "I am," and became self-aware.

"Then the Lord God said 'Behold, the man has become *like one of us*, knowing good and evil [polarity]. He must not be allowed to reach out his hand and take also from the tree of life and eat, and live forever.'"[7] Needless to say, the Lyran group was not pleased. In their anger they denied humans knowledge from the tree of life (Divine Heritage). The human race was thus forced to develop without the knowledge of its connection to the galactic family and the Whole. It would truly be a challenge.

To ensure that the humans did not seek this knowledge, the Lyran group employed some precautions. "...at the east of the garden He stationed the cherubim, and the flaming sword which turned every direction, to guard the way to the tree of life."[8] They left humanity its heritage—the legacy of Orion (symbolically portrayed as the sword), without leaving any knowledge of its resolution.

There are suggestions in the ancient Sumerian texts that the cherubim are actual mechanical or robotic devices which, in this case, protect the tree of life. What is the literal translation of the tree of life? In Sumerian the word for the tree of life was GISH.TIL. GISH meant a man-made device; TIL meant (and still does today in contemporary Hebrew) missile. Instead of an actual tree, this may mean the "vehicle to life"—or a spaceship. In Sumerian renderings there are clear depictions of rocketships, as well as men saluting these rocketships. It seems clear that the action by the gods of stationing the cherubim to keep humans from the tree of life was actually denying the humans the knowledge of their heritage. No longer would the Earth human be allowed to openly intermingle with the gods or leave the planet with them. Humans became banished from the heavens.

As an archetypal translation, Merlin can be analogous to the cherubim. He can hinder or help humanity, depending on the choices that are made. Merlin, in a sense, guards the way for us—to keep us from regressing into our planetary childhood. "He" is a bridge to the knowledge humanity seeks, a bridge across the torrid river of polarity. The "flaming sword" (the denied knowledge) is still too threatening.

Merlin continues to beckon humanity throughout eternity. He taunts the human race, speaking to the very depths of the human consciousness, asking that it claim the sword and cut through the illusion of Earth's perceived reality. He can be friend or foe, depending on one's orientation.

What happened to the Sirian group who interfered with the plans of the Lyrans? By interfering they became energetically tied to the development of Earth. They have always had many tricks up their sleeve, and in this case they got the last laugh. When working with the Lyran group during the genetic program, they inserted a latent DNA code within the human cells. This code is triggered by an accelerating vibration that occurs when a civilization begins to evolve spiritually. As Earth accelerates toward self-awareness and fourth density (which is occurring presently), the code is activated. Once activated, the human race unwinds its limited vision like a coil until the expanse of All That Is becomes visible. It was their way of allowing humanity to eat from the tree of life after all.

From these early seeders of planet Earth, humanity has been left a challenge. As stated, the "children" who are seeded usually carry the genetic codes and deep-seated attitudes of the "parents." If indeed Earth was seeded from a point of inequality and lack of free will, might this not explain why humans of many races today still carry an underlying belief in the superiority of the Caucasian/Aryan race (the Lyran group)? Could it be that the very roots of racial bigotry go as far back as the seeding of the planet? The earliest texts available to the seeker certainly suggest this. The Sumerian records give reference to the "black-headed ones" who worked the mines of Africa for the gods. If this is the case—that humanity carries the patterns of its forefathers— then this challenge is just beginning. Breaking free from this godspell that has been cast over humanity may be the key to the liberation of the human race on Earth.

In Earth's past the human race has received conflicting signals from the gods. There were times (some of which are recorded in the Sumerian texts such as the great flood) when humans were abandoned and left to die on the planet while the gods they trusted left in their rocketships. During these times some gods "illegally" rescued chosen humans. This has created an emotional encoding within the human species during times of crisis. The encoding remembers both of these patterns and a struggle is activated between the fear of abandonment and the joy of salvation. It is imperative that the human race resolve this dependence on the gods and become self-sufficient.

On present-day Earth, extraterrestrial groups whose encodings are rooted in the past still promise salvation. They come to humans as physical space beings or speak telepathically to those who can hear their frequency. Often they name various Earth humans as "commanders" or "chosen ones," and continue to tempt the human ego to perpetuate their *own* feelings of superiority. Though these off-planet groups mean well for the most part, they continually perpetuate the gap between the fear of abandonment and the joy of salvation, thus encouraging the separative belief in elitism. As humans take their own power and enter planetary adulthood, those remnant groups will transform as well. The majority of other extraterrestrial groups have learned from their past actions and desire a resolution of this conflict once and for all.

From the point of view of the Founders, the Plan was continuing perfectly. The Lyran group needed to play out the scenario for their own growth. These early extraterrestrial "gods" left behind clues on Earth that will eventually assist in awakening the planet to its heritage. As humanity awakens to this knowledge, it will begin to bring into play the tools that are needed to resolve the Orion drama. Resolution comes from allowance. If the human race can truly allow diversity within unity from a point of nonjudgment, Heaven on Earth *will* be created.

---

[1] These Lyrans, as well as others, have been known by the Hebrew term "Nefilim," erroneously translated as "giants." Nefilim literally means "those who have come down." Genesis 6:4 states: "The Nephilim were on the earth in those days—and also afterward—when the sons of God went to the daughters of men and had children by them. They were the heroes of old, men of renown." The original Hebrew term translated as "renown" is "shem," which literally means airborne vehicle, possibly rocketship. Hence, "They were the heroes of old, people of the rocketships."

[2] As implied previously, the Pleiadians carried Earth genetics that successfully integrated into the Lyran stock. Thus they became the ultimate choice to seed the terran race on Earth.

[3] Genesis 2:21.

[4] Genesis 2:16.

[5] The serpent is an archetypal symbol that is found in many ancient myths. The serpent's nature consistently portrays duality—it is feared but yet is a strong ally for humankind. In the Sumerian texts, Enki, the god (Sirian) who protects humanity, is also portrayed as a serpent. The judgment that the serpent is "evil" is more contemporary and may have been a ploy used by the gods (Lyrans) to keep humanity from following the instructions of the Sirians who were attempting to assist humankind.

[6] Genesis 3:4.

[7] Genesis 3:22.

[8] Genesis 3:24.

9

Zeta Reticuli: Transformation and Awakening

*"They seek the very depths of the soul.
They seek communion."*

—Whitley Strieber

The beginnings of the Zeta Reticuli civilization can be traced back in time to the inception of the Apex planet in the Lyran system by the Founders. Theirs is a unique and poignant development that has significant relevance to the evolution of planet Earth.

The Apex planet allowed polarity, expressed through extreme individualization, to tear them apart. Their technological evolution occurred rapidly, surpassing their spiritual development which prevented them from coexisting peacefully on their world. This imbalance in energy caused the virtual destruction of the Apex planet. From the view of an observer in space, the Apex world was obliterated. From the point of view of the Apex inhabitants, a different story occurred.

The Apex planet became extremely toxic. Pollution and high-level radiation made the planet's surface uninhabitable.

The Apexians who survived the catastrophe secluded themselves underground.[1] It was imperative that integration occur
within this new underground society, lest the cycle of destruction recreate itself. Recognizing its importance, they decided
to force integration (fusion) through a total restructuring of
their reality.

As the Apex planet approached its destruction, mentality
and intellect were so highly developed that it was becoming
noticeable in the physical forms of the Apexians. The
craniums had increased in size significantly over very few
generations. Natural childbirth became less and less successful because the craniums were not passing easily through the
birth canal. The females simply could not adapt to the
rapidity of cranial growth. Anticipating what may be a
species crisis, genetic engineers began learning cloning tech-
niques that could eventually replace the birth process. For
the Apexians, this move saved their species—for after the
planet's surface became uninhabitable, the Apexians found
themselves sterile.

Once they realized they were sterile, the Apexians decided
to use it to their advantage. They no longer wanted the type
of civilization they had had; they wanted to begin anew. Thus
they steadfastly decided to rigidly control the genetics of their
future society. Genetic engineers began work on the development of their new race. This race (they believed) would be
an integrated aspect of their past.

The first priority was to genetically alter the brain structures to affect emotional expression. They shunned their past
expression of passion and chaos; they now wanted order.
They brain was thus altered to output a consistent chemical
response to external stimuli. They achieved detachment from
their ego structure. Over generations of neurochemical
manipulations, the Apexians became a group mind. The

individualistic expressions they were once extremely proud of were now gone.

The combination of planetary radiation and the effects of their cloning began to produce a race with little physical variance from one person to the other. In order to utilize the planet's underground environment more efficiently, their bodies were created smaller in stature. In adaptation to the absence of ultraviolet light and natural sunlight, their eyes began to respond to different frequencies of the visual spectrum. Their pupils mutated to cover the entire eye, and the eyes enlarged to allow more surface space for gathering light.

In response to the lack of fresh food, their bodies eventually adapted to the absorption of certain frequencies of light as nourishment. Their skin became photothermic and photovoltaic, sensitive to light sources in the underground caverns. Salvaged plants and luminiferous underground minerals aided in their nourishment. Many of their organs, such as those of the digestive and reproductive systems, thus began to atrophy. The transformation they underwent touched every aspect of their beings. A new civilization began to emerge.

The force and vibration of the Apexians' previous atomic blasts eventually folded the space surrounding the Apex planet and they emerged "on the other side" of a dimensional doorway. During the underground seclusion which lasted thousands of years, the Apexians had no idea that their planet had changed its position in time and space. It wasn't until they emerged onto the planet's surface environment generations later that they found the star field had shifted dramatically. It was then that they knew the extent of their actions. The Apex planet had shifted its position (relative to time and space) in the cosmos. It now existed "slightly off" in dimension compared to the worlds they were familiar with. To understand what had occurred and use the knowledge to their benefit, they began to master the science of folding time and space.

The day they finally emerged onto the planet's surface once again, they had become a new species. Like a phoenix rising from the ashes, they had managed to produce transformation from destruction. They were no longer Apexians. They now assumed a new identity, that of One People Reflecting the Whole.

From Earth's point of view, these One People are now called the Zeta Reticuli.[2] Their planet, through its shift in dimension, inserted itself into the binary system of Zeta Reticuli 1 and Zeta Reticuli 2 [3] in the Reticulum Rhomboidalis star group.[4] From that base they began reestablishing their connections with the Founders of Life. To this day they continue to carry out the wishes of the Founders for galactic evolution. What they are just beginning to realize is that they are carrying out their own evolution as well.

The Reticuli require a way to strengthen their genetic line to create a future for their race. After generations of cloning using the same genetic material, they became severely inbred and stagnant in their evolutionary growth. Their race is dying, but their oversoul wishes to continue incarnating in physicality. They are deliberately keeping themselves from transitioning to fifth density in order to leave behind a seed of themselves that can genetically continue to reproduce. This will aid the galactic whole in its evolution.

Recognizing their predicament, they called out to the Founders.

The Founders introduced the Reticuli to a diverse planet that genetically possessed a gene pool from every human species since the inception of the Lyran races. Instead of the Reticuli going from civilization to civilization gathering genetic material, they could now get it in one place. This planet is Earth.

The Reticuli were primarily attracted to Earth in the 1940s, when the planet began to possess the technology to self-destruct. They are quite aware that their past represents a future possibility for Earth. Because of their ability to travel through time, they could have gathered genetic material from any time in Earth's past. However, they needed genetic material from a period of Earth's history when civilization stands on the brink of destruction and transformation. This will aid them in their own integrative process. In a sense, it is their way of *changing* their past. By interacting with present-day Earth, they heal their past and change their future.

Today on Earth they carry out this genetic program. Since this planet has not yet understood or embraced the idea of soul choice, most of the individuals who are participants in this genetic program consider themselves victims. There are thousands of stories of terrorized abductees who are plagued by reoccurring experiences of extraterrestrials who snatch them from their warm beds.[5] Experiences of terror occur because humanity is not yet willing to face its own shadow, which is reflected in the mirror that the Reticuli represent.

The Reticuli primarily seek specific human characteristics that they bred *out* of their race eons ago. One such characteristic is a variability of reaction to external stimuli. To relearn this, they must sample and study human neurochemical reactions to a myriad of stimuli.

Their most common method of studying these neurochemical secretions is by the implantation of an organic probe. These probes are inserted into the head of the abductee through either the nose, eye, or ear cavity. These probes absorb and catalog neurochemical data and are removed periodically for study and then reinserted. Should an individual die, the organic probe can be naturally absorbed by the body.

Not only are they seeking biological information from humans, but they are also seeking emotional learning as well. It has been eons since they parented children. The human nurturing ability is a fascination to them. As they begin altering their neurochemical structures, they will once again be able to respond maternally to their progeny. This is one of the primary reasons why women are abducted and asked to hold hybrid children. These human females are helping to reawaken the maternal and procreational instincts of the Zeta Reticuli.

Humanity is not only helping *them*—*they* are playing a vital role for Earth as well. The Founders are well aware that Earth's humanity *must* integrate itself on several levels or the scenario will continue. The Reticuli reflect to the human race one of the most fundamental ideas that it has denied—unity. Humans reflect to the Reticuli their own individuality, which terrifies them. If the gap created by humanity's fears can be bridged, transformation will occur in a most profound way.

The Reticuli are presently acquiring genetic material from *volunteers* who have, on a soul level, agreed to be a part of the awakening of the Earth and the birth of a new civilization. At this stage of the game, fear is still needed on the part of the abductees. On Earth, fear is a primary obstacle to growth. If humanity can move through fear, it will achieve many goals that presently seem out of reach. It will be done through awareness, *not* through the validation of victimhood. The Reticuli need to confront their fear as well (which they still deny), and move through it. Without that fear, growth would be minimal. Sometimes the greatest barriers produce the greatest rewards.

One of these rewards is the creation of a new hybrid race who possess the integrated qualities of the Zeta Reticuli and the Earth human. They will be unified and diverse. They will be rich with humor and fluid with their emotions. Most of all, they will be the unconditionally loving heralds who lead us back to the Source of All.

---

[1]This underground seclusion produced various factions of Apexians. The one explored in the present chapter is a more benign race. Others who were more negatively oriented (and assisted in creating the chaos on the Apex planet) eventually left the Apex planet after thousands of years and settled in areas of Sirius and Orion, most notably Betelgeuse. The negative beings who have present interaction with Earth have been labeled as the negative Sirians and the Greys; they have their own motivations for their interactions with Earth.

[2]As stated in footnote 1, there were many factions of Apexians who went underground. While underground, one faction developed themselves in a similar manner as the *benign* Zeta Reticuli. The faction under discussion can be considered the negative Zeta Reticuli, who, after the shift into the Reticulum star system, left the original Apex planet and colonized another planet in the Zeta Reticuli binary system. They are nearly identical in appearance and can be differentiated only by their vibration or behavior, which is inherently negative in nature.

Another possibility is that perhaps when contradicting versions of the Zeta Reticuli are seen, humans are actually interacting with the Reticuli from different evolutionary points in their history, though they all come from *Earth's* future. The more negative manifestations might be their past, whereas some of the more harmless interactions might occur from a further evolved state. When they come to humans in the present, it is assumed that they originate from a single point in time. If they are indeed coming to Earth from various points in their development, it would explain the wide range of reported abduction experiences conducted by the same beings.

[3]Webster's Dictionary defines "reticular" as "like a network; complicated." Some may surely attest that the psyche of the Zeta Reticuli
beings is complicated indeed!

[4]One of the most famous early cases of UFO abduction that supports
the origin of these beings is the Betty and Barney Hill case. In 1961
Betty Hill was shown a map of a star group during her abduction.
Years later she drew this map while under hypnosis. At the time, there
was no reference to this group on known star charts. It has since been
discovered that Betty's drawing matches a newly discovered star group
seen from Earth's southern hemisphere. The star group, Reticulum
Rhomboidalis (the Rhomboidal Net) houses the binary star group now
labeled Zeta Reticuli 1 and 2.

[5]Although most abductions are carried out by the Zeta Reticuli, there
are isolated incidents of other groups using the abduction scenario for
their own purposes. For example, the negatively oriented Sirians,
Orions, and those termed the "Greys" very often use terrorizing
methods. It is essential that humans learn to differentiate the Zeta
Reticuli contact from the more malevolent interactions.

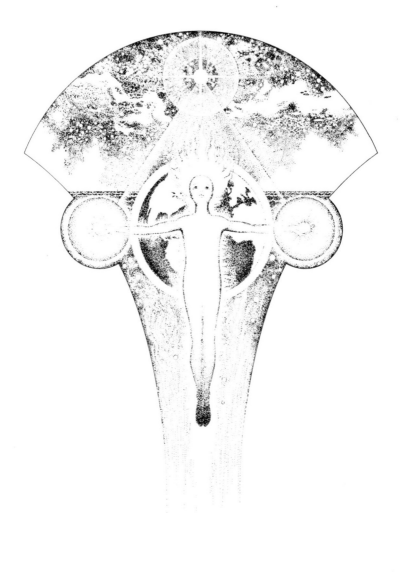

10

Integration: Coming Home to Ourselves

"And while all other creatures from their birth
With downcast eyes gaze on their kindred earth;
He bids man walk erect, and scan the heaven
From whence his soul has sprung,
to which his hopes are given."

—Ovid

Integration means the allowance of all levels of being as valid portions of the whole. It means letting go of denial. It means embracing ourselves as well as each other.

Just as our unified consciousness *created* this realm of polarity, we can transform it. When integration occurs, this realm will become defined by very different parameters. We will become the archetypes as well as the Founders. We will shift perspective and become conscious of ourselves as the Creator. It does not necessarily mean that our identities will be absorbed. It could mean that we will awaken to the point where we will consciously choose our destinies. Perhaps we may choose to enter other realms and be the unseen friends for planets still playing the game of separation. We

may even be another planet's extraterrestrials—pondering the
same decisions regarding interference that our forefathers
faced.

In stilling ourselves and listening closely, we can hear and
feel the undercurrents of this transformation. Existence and
change are the only constants. We can play the game of
illusion that we are an accidental creation, but sooner or later
we tap ourselves on our shoulder and the game is up. In
Earth's reality we have created the Arcturans, Sirians, Lyrans,
Orions, Reticuli, Pleiadians, etc., to be the selves that tap us
on the shoulder. They are really part of the same one thing—
us.

So how on Earth do we encourage integration to take
place? First of all, *we must know that it will take place with
or without our conscious action. The difference is only that
conscious action will allow the ride to be more enjoyable. We
will feel more in control of our destinies.*

The conscious action that will accelerate our integration
process is very simple—allowance. If we *allow* on all levels
in which the integration takes place, we will see our paths
unfold before us joyously.

Integration will take place on four main levels: Mental,
Emotional, Spiritual, and Physical.

Mental

For us to integrate our mentality means that we allow
ourselves to combine not only our cerebral processes, but our
intuitive and emotional ones as well. The kind of thought
today that is validated most is almost entirely head-centered.
Formulas and calculations determine the reality of twentieth
century Earth. If we can allow ourselves to understand that
the intuitive and emotional processes are just as valid and can

be used in combination with the mental, we will be well on our way toward integrating our mentality.

Emotional

Integrating emotionally means that we begin learning how to embrace our shadow self. We can start opening inner closets and digging deep into the subconscious for beliefs that hold us back. More often than not, these neglected parts of ourselves only want attention. As the Pleiadians and the Lyrans before them discovered, denial only prolongs the pain of existence. Let us learn from these other selves on distant worlds. Let us not repeat the same lessons over and over again.

Spiritual

To integrate spiritually is perhaps the easiest of all. Each person possesses an inner spirituality that is not connected to doctrine. If we can release the doctrine and touch the innate spirituality, we begin the integration process. It extends outward onto the planet by the honoring of *every person's truth* as a manifestation of the One Truth. This allows each of us to coexist within our philosophies without needing to change each other's beliefs. The fact that God/All That Is exists is not changed by our argument over which color robe "He" wears. We are so afraid of being alone and separate that we create even more separation through our desire to have a unified doctrine. If we have the courage to begin touching this inner spirituality, we will see our transformation blossom.

Physical

Integration physically is slight different. It involves an acknowledgment of our past and our history as being part of a grander scenario on a cosmic scale. From the Source and the Founders we fragmented. We have stretched our in-dividualization to its outer limits. Coming together will require us to once again acknowledge and accept ourselves as part of our galactic family. As we move through our racial fear and stop allowing skin color and outer differences to be barriers between us, we also move through our fear by celebrating the communion that the Zeta Reticuli offer us. We can allow integration on all levels into our physical life here on Earth.

Not one of us is "from" another place. We are from the Source, and the Source is vast. To say we are "from" the Pleiades is a denial of all the other ideas that we are. Our terrestrial selves become confused if we continually deny that our existence is part of the planet's body. We are of All That Is! If we feel a connection to an off-planet race, we are identifying with what they represent or with various lives we have lived in that system. If individuals insist on stating they are "from" somewhere, the suggestion is offered that they proclaim their alliance with Earth. They have chosen a life *here*. In a very real sense, Earth people can be seen as models for integration. We are divine and terrestrial; of gods and men. We are proof positive that human life can adapt to seemingly insurmountable circumstances. Let us celebrate *humanity!*

There are no space brothers who are *really* going to save us—they are too busy saving themselves! We are not children. Though we are still somewhat playing the game of unawareness, we are looked at by other civilizations as an enigma. We are the civilization that refused to die! Our resilience and faith in our abilities has continually proven our worth. We refused to be dominated and used by the Lyran group in the Garden of Eden. Various "plagues" by the gods have not succeeded in wiping us out. Thanks to Noah and the Sirian overlord who warned him, we have a flourishing civilization today.

Many have wondered why Earth has been observed by so many extraterrestrial groups. Perhaps we are a predictable demonstration of integration in action. It may be painful, but in our mass conscious belief, pain can produce miraculous results.

Earth of the present and Earth of the future is indeed that miracle. Let us celebrate that miracle by integrating ourselves and taking responsibility for our planetary reality. We are part of an Association of Worlds and our membership is up for renewal! This time, membership requires our awakening to the cosmic drama we've agreed to be a part of. Our awakening will lead us home...to ourselves.

Glossary of Terms

Abductions: From the point of view of an abductee, this is the unwilling detainment by various extraterrestrial groups for the purposes of: (1) Study; (2) Genetic sampling; (3) Tracking of genetic family histories; (4) Maintaining and developing hybridization programs; (5) Human maternal response observation; (6) Observation of neurological responses to emotional stimuli; (7) Communication; and other purposes including (8) The instillment of fear and terror, which is believed by the negatively oriented extraterrestrials to halt the development or acceleration of the abductees and of the mass consciousness. Listed are some groups involved in abductions and their primary reasons for interaction.

Zeta Reticuli: #1, 2, 3, 4, 5, 6, 7
Physical Sirians (negative): #1, 2, 3, 8
Pleiadians: #1, 3, 6, 7
Greys: #8
Physical Orions (negative): #8

Adam: This is the label given to the first stable prototype model of Homo sapiens. Adam comes from the Hebrew "Adama," meaning "created of the Earth's soil," thus "earthling." In Sumerian the word is "Adapa," meaning "model man."

All That Is: This is a term that many use in place of "God" or the "Creator," because it includes the observer as part of the Creator.

Altair: Altair, whose civilization was colonized from Vega, lies 15 and 1/5 light years from Earth. Altair's magnitude is 1.3 and its color pale yellow. The Altair civilization is quiet and contemplative, given to peaceful philosophic orientation. They are not currently involved in space exploration.

Andromeda: (Messier 31) Andromeda is a large spiral galaxy and is the closest to the Milky Way at a distance of 2.2 million light years. The nature of the Andromeda realm is abstract and fluid. A dimensional doorway exists in our nearby galactic neighborhood as a bridge to the Andromeda energy. This bridge/doorway is the star Antares.

Angels/Angelic Kingdom: Existing within the realms of fifth and sixth density, the angelic kingdom has interacted with Earth through various means. These include spirit-guide manifestation, visions, inspiration, channeling, and telepathic communication. Energies appearing as angels are frequently from the Arcturus realm.

Antares: Lying in the Scorpius constellation, Antares is considered a binary star of fiery red and emerald green. Antares is the interdimensional bridge to Andromeda from our galaxy. Some souls, upon physical incarnation, choose to pass through the Antares gateway to reactivate soul memory.

Anubis: In ancient Egypt, Anubis was considered a guide of the underworld. His usual form is that of a crouching desert dog or jackal. He was known to lead souls through the astral (as in dream state) as well as to Amenti, or land of the dead. It is interesting how the prefix "an" in both Sumerian and Egyptian means "of Heaven." Anubis (Anpu in Egyptian) and Anu (Sumerian) both possessed the symbology of the jackal or dog, suggesting a direct connection to the Dog Star Sirius.

Apex Planet, Apexians: The Apex planet was one of the first developed societies in the Lyra star group. After its planetary catastrophe the Apex planet was shifted dimensionally into another region of space/time. They eventually became the race of the Zeta Reticuli.

Archetype: The Living Webster Encyclopedic Dictionary defines archetype as "model or first form; the original pattern after which a thing is made, or to which it corresponds." This definition suggest that all of our archetypal ideas are inherent patterns (dating from the birth of the galactic humanity) that continue to evolve. New symbols of these patterns are being found, but the innate properties are the same.

Arcturus: Arcturus is seen as a golden yellow star, with a magnitude of 0.3. Its energy works with humanity as an emotional and spiritual healer. It is also an energy gateway through which humans pass upon death and birth. It functions as a way station for nonphysical consciousness to become accustomed to physicality.

Arcturus/Sirius Matrix: The combined energies of Arcturus and Sirius provide a balance of physical, emotional, and spiritual healing. This matrix has been tapped into by humanity since its inception and has been known through many archetypal ideas.

Association of Worlds: The Association is a group of physical and nonphysical beings from many realms who come together for many purposes. Some have called them a galactic confederation or federation. There is no hierarchical structure or authority inherent in the Association. The primary purposes for their interactions with Earth are: (1) to gently nudge humanity toward a greater awareness of itself and its place within the Association and (2) to prevent a critical number of nuclear explosions on Earth, which can cause a rip in the fabric of space/time, affecting the galactic neighborhood. They have absolutely no intention now of evacuating anyone from Earth under any conditions. They understand the absolute necessity for the human race to become responsible for itself.

Atlantis: This was the combined extraterrestrial/human cultural period prior to the flood. The flood occurred in approximately 11,000 B.C.

Australopithecus: This term denotes any hominid of the extinct genus Australopithecus of the Pleistocene epoch. Advanced Australopithecus is the first being considered to be truly manlike, existing some 2 million years ago.

Bipedal: Any being possessing two feet can be considered bipedal.

Black Hole: A star becomes a black hole when it has collapsed and reaches such a high density that its gravitational field exceeds the escape velocity of even light photons. Astronomers theorize that a change in space/time occurs. This creates many probabilities, including (1) entrance and exit points to other dimensional realities; (2) birthplaces of future stars; (3) an ability to harness the powers of time travel; and (4) an entrance into an antimatter universe.

Black League: The Black League was an organizational resistance pattern developed during the Orion conflicts to counter the efforts of the Orion Empire, which was attempting physical and spiritual domination of the entire region. The Black League manifested not only as underground paramilitary resistance organizations but as a spiritual and philosophical orientation that manifested in many forms. These patterns have attempted balance in other planetary systems and are presently playing out on Earth as well as through its reincarnational cycle.

Cetaceans: Cetaceans are a marine mammal of the order "cetacea" that includes whales, dolphins, and porpoises. Cetaceans possess consciousness of the same type as humans, and are considered by extraterrestrials to be "water humans."

Channeling: Channeling is the process of receiving communication from an infinite number of dimensional realities. This communication can be expressed via writing, verbal relay, artwork, music composition, and any creative expression.

Cherubim: The most ancient references concerning forms of cherubim (in the Akkadian and Sumerian records) describe a mechanical security device (i.e., robot) that was used to secure the highly sensitive areas of the gods to which humans were denied access. This idea later evolved into a more abstract and spiritual one, displayed in the archetypal manifestation of a winged celestial figure who guards sacred places and who is a servant of God.

Christ Consciousness: The Christ Consciousness is the aspect of a mass consciousness that recognizes itself as a single being. This can be equated with a sixth-density vibration.

Cloning: Cloning is an asexual method for reproduction that uses an original seed or genetic stock for replication.

Consciousness: Consciousness is the underlying binding force of all creation. It exists in infinite manifestations and may defy definition.

Cro-Magnon: Cro-Magnon was a group of tall, erect, prehistoric people who used bone and stone implements. Thirty-five thousand years ago this new race of beings (identified with the larger type Homo sapiens, or "thinking man") appeared seemingly out of nowhere and coexisted for a period of time with the dying race of the Neanderthal.

Crystal Skull: Found in southern Mexico, the skull is carved out of crystal in the shape of a human cranium. The most well-known skull is presently the property of Anna

Mitchell-Hedges. Many claim to have mystical or paranormal experiences when they are in the skull's presence.

Density: Density denotes a vibrational frequency and not a location, which the term "dimension" implies. The density structure of this reality is primarily expressed in seven levels, though each level has sublevels within it. The density scale is a model used to communicate one's perception of orientation in relation to other realities.

Devic: In Sanskrit, deva means a god or divinity; one of an order of good spirits. In Western mysticism, the devic energy is the spirit consciousness of mineral, plant, animal and more subtle forms such as fairies.

Dimension: Dimension refers to one's location in space/time rather than a person's vibrational frequency (density). Webster defines "dimension" as: "Magnitude measured in a particular direction, specifically length, breadth, thickness or time." There are an infinite number of dimensions existing within a given density or vibrational frequency.

Dimensional Infusion: God—The Whole, All That Is— became curious about the idea of separation and created a realm in which to explore it. This was achieved by creating the boundaries of dimension. One may equate the Dimensional Infusion with the process of creation itself.

DNA: DNA is the abbreviation for deoxyribonucleic acid which is a compound found in chromosomes and consists of a long chain molecule comprising many repeated and varied combinations of four nucleotides, one of which is the sugar deoxyribose; subdivisions of the molecule are believed to be the genes. DNA is the major repository of genetic information.

Dogon: The Dogon people are an African tribe living in the Mali Republic (western Africa) near Timbuktu, thought to have migrated from Egypt. For many generations they have possessed a knowledge of advanced astrophysics concerning the Sirius star system that they claim was given to them by beings from that system.

Easter Island: Easter Island is located in the Pacific between Chile and French Polynesia and is known for the mysterious statues of humanoid beings left scattered throughout the island.

Ego: Ego is the "I" or self as distinguished from the selves of others. It is that part of the psyche that is conscious in physical reality and acts as the mediator between inner and outer worlds.

Enki: In Sumerian, Enki means "Lord of Earth" and is considered to be the one who imparts the knowledge of civilization to mankind. He was also known to the Babylonians as "Oannes," and to the Egyptians as "Ptah." He is the god of wisdom and knowledge, and throughout time his symbol has been the snake. According to the Sumerian texts, Enki is the one who instructs Noah to build an ark so that humanity can be saved. This was in direct defiance of the orders of Enlil, who desired the destruction of humanity.

Enlil: In Sumerian Enlil means "Lord of the Air" and was considered to be the chief of all the lands. The Sumerians considered him to be supreme. Enki and Enlil were half-brothers who had the same father, each claiming to be the firstborn, which caused each to believe he was the ruling deity. This conflict is thought to be the source of many later conflicts between the gods.

Etheric: Etheric pertains to an environment that is not based on physical reality but still contains form. Many ideas or thoughtforms in the etheric may become manifest in the physical world.

Eve: Eve was the first female prototype created from the cloning or gene splicing of the male humanoid prototype called Adam. This pertains to Homo sapiens only.

Excalibur: The word means "beyond calibration," and thus beyond measure. It is the legendary sword of the kings of the ancient Celtic peoples. Archetypally it is an Orion manifestation of the power and liberation of truth, which can cut through all illusion.

Founders: The Founders are the collective soul of the humanoid family. To physical beings they manifest in humanoid form—tall, graceful, androgynous—appearing somewhat insectlike. Humanity is the result of the internal fragmentation of the Founders.

Frequency: Matter is vibrating energy. Different vibratory rates denote the properties of matter. Frequency is the rate at which molecules or consciousness vibrates.

Future Selves: Because the past, present, and future exist simultaneously, a being may contact parts of itself across the expanse of time. Extraterrestrials will often contact their past selves (such as Earth) to create a connection, and this can often heal their own past. The idea of "higher selves" and "future selves" can be interchangeable in that a future self is an evolved version of the present or past self.

Galactic Family: The galactic family is the group of extraterrestrial beings (physical and nonphysical) who are interrelated energetically and/or physically with Earth's development. These include: the Lyran races, Arcturus, Sirius, the Pleiadian races, Zeta Reticuli, Orion, and many others not mentioned.

Homo: Homo (Latin for "man") denotes a genus of the order of primates which includes all races of modern man (Homo sapiens) and various extinct species.

Homo sapiens: Homo sapiens is the single surviving species of human evolutionary development, or modern man, belonging to the genus Homo and the primate family Hominidae. The account in *Genesis* of the creation of man refers to the creation of Homo sapiens, not of other extinct species such as Neanderthal.

Human: Webster defines "human" as "akin to humus, the ground; having the qualities or attributes of man." This can be expanded by saying that the term "human" refers specifically to the Earth human, who is a subset of the larger humanoid family of the Lyran forefathers.

Humanoid: Humanoid as used in the text refers to anyone of Lyran descent.

Hybrid: A hybrid is anything derived from heterogeneous sources or composed of elements of different or incongruous kinds. The hybrids spoken of in UFO literature are primarily a cross between the Earth human and Zeta Reticuli beings. The specific process that is used to create these hybrids has not yet been revealed. It uses not only genetic splicing and cloning, but a form of light-plasma engineering technology with which humans are unfamiliar.**Id:** Freud defines the id as being the part of the personality structure that is primitive, instinctual, childish, and obeys the pleasure principle. The qualities of the id can be likened to the humans' passage through second-density reality in the early stages of life.

Illuminati: Webster defines "illuminati" as "persons possessing, or alleging to possess, superior enlightenment; a name for various sects or societies which claim to possess superior enlightenment." This may refer to humans as well as various extraterrestrial groups (physical or nonphysical) who are either self-deluded or who deliberately attempt to gain control of human society. Some such negative groups include: Orions, Sirians, Lyrans, and "renegade" Pleiadians. The historical foundation of the Illuminati is rooted in times past when various extraterrestrial groups were in control (or fighting for control) of the Earth in whole or in part. Because of these ancient interactions, the Illuminati believe that they have territorial rights over the Earth that they still disagree about amongst themselves. Some will attempt incarnation in order to carry their wishes out in the physical. The Illuminati can also be viewed from the nonphysical as an archetypal energy that once interacted physically with Earth. This group eventually side-stepped natural evolution and became a specifically focused archetype. This archetype is bound tightly with the planet by its need to keep humans from their natural evolutionary processes.

Incarnate: The act of incarnation (as the term is used) is the process whereby a soul will embody itself in a physical vehicle in a separative density such as the third or fourth. The created illusion is that there is a memory loss of the greater identity of an individual consciousness.

Inception: The term "Inception" is used in the text to denote the beginning point of Homo sapiens on Earth.

Isis: In ancient Egypt Isis was known as the wife/sister of Osiris, sister of Nephthys, and mother of Horus. She is featured prominently in Egyptian mythology as a goddess of immense magical power and as the archetypal maternal figure. Other cultures have known her as Ishtar (Semites), Athena (Greeks), Kwan Yin (Chinese), and Inanna (Sumerians).

Karma: Karma denotes balance and is a principle carried within the soul's energy from lifetime to lifetime. The old way of understanding was that karma was balanced through "an eye for an eye." A more multidimensional perspective claims that karma is superseded by the exercising of free will and choice along with the commitment to the practicing of one's highest truths. Karma can be carried by an individual, a group, a species, or a mass consciousness.

Lemuria: Lemuria was a continent and a cultural period that predated and overlapped Atlantis. It was located in the Pacific region of Earth and is thought to have been the first culture influenced by extraterrestrial sources.

Lenticular Clouds: Lenticular clouds have the form of a double convex lens or a lentil. Often their breathtaking appearance is similar to a saucer-shaped spacecraft. Although nature is often behind such a cloud formation, sometimes the physical environment will translate extraterrestrial energy or consciousness into this form.

Lyra: The constellation of Lyra has long been recognized in Earth's myths. Some have even connected it with the Pleiades (for example, Ovid, who mentioned that the seven strings of Lyra equaled the number of the Pleiades). This can be considered the birthplace or womb of the humanoid race within Earth's area of the Milky way. All subspecies such as Sirius, Orion, Earth, Pleiades, Centauri, Altair (and many lesser-known groups) are descendants of the Lyran races.

Lyran Group: The Lyran group is referred to as the original seeders of humanoid life on Earth. In the text it refers to the forefather race of other groups such as the Pleiades and Sirius, as well as the first fragmentation from the Founders of Life.

Macrocosm: Macrocosm refers to a large-scale model of a smaller unit. An example is the solar system representing the structure of atomic particles.

Mass Consciousness: Mass consciousness refers to the singular identity of a group. For example, the mass consciousness of Earth is made up of each individual consciousness integrated into a homogeneous unit.

Matrix: (from Latin: Mater/Mother) Matrix is that which originates, develops, or encloses anything; a network of ideas that forms a symbiotic relationship; an archetypal template.

Meier, (Billy) Eduard: The Swiss Billy Meier is known to possess the most extensive contact notes from repeated interactions with Pleiadian beings, among others. Numerous photographs have been taken that clearly show spacecraft in detail.

Men in Black: Also known as "MIBs," these beings are known as terrorizers of UFO contactees. They are described as being tall and wearing dark clothing. They have been seen with slightly oriental features and often wear dark glasses. Their apparent purpose is to frighten contactees into silence about their experiences and knowledge. Originally thought to be government agents, other ideas have presently surfaced such as: thoughtforms, androids, and negatively oriented extraterrestrials (Orions, Sirians, and Greys). One or all of the above ideas (in various combinations) can be correlated with the MIB identity.

Meta-atomic: Meta-atomic refers to the idea of beyond subatomic. The template that defines the subatomic nature exists on a meta-atomic level.

Microcosm: Microcosm means anything regarded as a world in miniature. An example of this is how atomic structure relates to the structure of the solar system.

Multidimensional: A multidimensional idea is one that possesses many dimensions. Humans are referred to as multidimensional because they exist on many dimensional levels as yet unseen or unmeasurable.

Neanderthal: Neanderthal refers to a paleolithic cave dweller of the Late Pleistocene epoch, Homo neanderthalensis, whose bones have been found in parts of Europe, Africa, and Asia. The remains of the Neanderthal have been dated at approximately 100,000 years ago. They seem to have evolved out of Homo erectus and then died out during the appearance of Homo sapiens 35,000 years ago.

Noah: Noah is a Semitic derivative of the much earlier Sumerian name "Utnapishtim" and the Akkadian "Ziusudra." The writings of these civilizations all portray a Noahlike character who is warned of the flood by the god Enki. The Genesis story of the flood is a condensation of much earlier and much more detailed pre-Biblical accounts in Sumerian and Akkadian literature.

Octave: Octave is the eighth of seven steps; it is the integration of seven levels. As it is used in the text, it refers to a realm of existence that consciousness will move into after integrating the seven densities.

Orion: The constellation of Orion is a pattern of stars that has intrigued mankind since ancient times. The word Orion may derive from the ancient Akkadian word "Uru-anna," which means "the light of heaven." Western cultures have often identified this constellation as the hunter. The inherent energy of Orion is associated with polarity conflict. Earth is presently attempting a final integration of these polarities, hence the strong feelings of connection that many humans display regarding Orion.

Orion Light: The term "Orion Light" refers to the point in Orion's evolution where they have succeeded in integrating polarity. It can also be considered the Orion mass consciousness—the nonphysical aspect of Orion that operates from a sense of unity and integration.

Osiris: Osiris is considered one of the principle Egyptian gods. He has been referred to as "he who dwells in Orion with a season in the sky and a season on Earth," among other epithets. Whatever his identity, most ancient writings strongly point to his extraterrestrial origin.

Photothermic: Photothermic involves both light and heat. In their underground caverns the Apexians/Zeta Reticuli mutated to convert certain frequencies of light into heat.

Photovoltaic: Photovoltaic refers to the idea of providing a source of electric current from light or similar radiation. In the underground caverns the Apexians/Zeta Reticuli mutated to the point where they could convert certain frequencies of light and radiation into electrical energy.

Pleiades: The Pleiades group is an open star cluster in the constellation Taurus, existing approximately 500 light years from Earth. There are 250-500 stars within the cluster, although only nine have been named. Most ancient cultures claim seven stars. These include China, who called them the "Seven Sisters of Industry," and Greece, who referred to them as the "Seven Daughters of Atlas." More than any other star group, the Pleiades has captured the attention of both ancient and modern civilizations.

Polarity/Polarization: Polarity refers to the presence or manifestation of two opposite (or contrasting) principles or tendencies. Polarization is the production of the state of polarity, where rays of light or energy exhibit different properties in different directions.

Prism: A prism is a transparent body with a triangular base used to polarize or decompose light or energy into its spectrum.

Prism of Lyra: This is the archetypal idea of the entrance of consciousness into this reality. For Earth's galactic family the entrance point exists within the Lyran system. As consciousness/energy emerged, it fragmented into seven density frequencies, much as a prism would fragment light into seven visible colors.

Prototype: A prototype is an original model on which something is formed; an archetype; a form on which a group is based. In the text the term/name "Adam" is used to denote the prototype on which Homo sapiens in based.

Reticuli: As used in the text, Reticuli refers to the beings from the star system Zeta Reticuli.

Reticulum Rhomboidalis: This star group lies north of Hydrus and the Greater Cloud and contains thirty-four stars from magnitudes of 3.3 to 7. The binary system of Zeta Reticuli 1 and Zeta Reticuli 2 are present in this formation and are seen only from the southern hemisphere of Earth.

Science of Chaos: The study of apparent random motion that reveals a much deeper level of order below the superficial observation is referred to as the Science of Chaos.

Semjase: Semjase was the name of the female Pleiadian cosmonaut who served as Billy Meier's primary contact.

Set: (Also spelled as: Seth, Setekh, Setesh, Suty, or Sutekh.) Generally speaking, in Egyptian mythology Set is seen as the god of chaotic forces and violence. There has been considerable controversy over his actual role in ancient Egypt. The temples and priesthoods of Set are mentioned in the text in reference to the worship of dark forces.

Sirian Group: As used in the text, the Sirian group refers to a group of extraterrestrials (not necessarily all from Sirius) who were instrumental in the inception of Earth and the development of the human race.

Sirius: Sirius is a member of the constellation Canis Major, known as the Dog Star. It lies 8.7 light years from Earth and is the most brilliant star (as distinguished from planets) observed by the naked eye.

Social Memory Complex: This term refers to a mass consciousness or a nonphysical group-matrix identity that has evolved from a physical society.

Soul Braiding: A soul braid is the most common form of what has been labeled "walk-in." It occurs when a physical individual takes in more of their own higher, future, or parallel energy and incorporates it into their own personality and physiological life.

Sumerian: The Sumerians were a people who comprised one of Earth's oldest known civilizations (approximately 4,000 B.C.), located in southern Mesopotamia (Iraq/Iran). They were a non-Semitic people of unknown origin. They claimed to have had the foundation of their civilization given to them by the "DIN.GIR"—pure ones of the bright-pointed objects, or people of the fiery rockets—or, in human terms, extraterrestrials.

Superego: Freud defined the superego as a system within the mind which, acting consciously or unconsciously, brings perceived parental, social, or moral standards to bear upon the actions and decisions of the ego. As used in the text, the superego is equated with the higher aspect of consciousness that is the nexus for the integration of personality.

Time: Time can be considered a specific continuum where the relationship of movement and speed are measured through linear means.

Tree of the Knowledge of Good and Evil: Referred to in the book of Genesis, it is the tree in the Garden of Eden whose fruit God forbade Adam and Eve to eat from. As used in the text, the tree of the knowledge of good and evil symbolizes the knowledge of polarity.

Tree of Life: In the book of Genesis Adam and Eve were banished from Eden and forbidden to eat from the tree of life, which would give them immortality. As used in the text, the tree of life represents knowledge of the divine relationship between human beings and the Creator—thus revealing that our spirituality is not dependent upon those who genetically engineered us.

Vega: Vega is the alpha star in the constellation of Lyra (even though it is actually closer to Earth than the other star systems in the Lyran constellation). Vega was one of the first Lyran civilizations to develop a unique and cohesive identity which assisted in seeding and colonizing many systems, including Altair, Centauri, Sirius, and Orion.

Walk-In: Generally, a walk-in experience will take two forms. The most common can be considered a soul braid in which more of an individual's own energy (higher self or future aspects) is brought in and integrated with the personality. The second and more rare is an instance in which an actual "separate" consciousness inhabits a human body while the original soul departs the physical plane. This is a highly personal experience where the newly arrived entity does not need to proclaim its origin or status. Quite frequently the soul-braid experience is mistaken for the walk-in exchange because the personality construct (as biochemically encoded within the brain) experiences much the same manifestation in either case.

White Hole: As used in the text, a white hole is an emergence point for consciousness and energy.

Zeta Reticuli: Discovered in the late 1960s, this binary star group is located in the Reticulum constellation, which is seen from Earth's southern hemisphere. As used in the text, the Reticuli are a race with many subgroups who are conducting the primary genetic experiments and abductions on present-day Earth humans. Their average height is three and one-half feet. They have large craniums and extremely large eyes. Their sex is indistinguishable. Overall their intent is benign, despite the trauma that many individuals experience in their presence.

Selected Bibliography

Anka, Darryl. *The New Metaphysics.* Light and Sound Communications, 1986.

Burnham Jr., Robert. *Burnham's Celestial Handbook, Vols. 1, 2, and 3.* Dover Publications, 1978.

Cott, Jonathan. *The Search for Omm Sety.* Doubleday, 1987.

Dickinson, Terence. *The Zeta Reticuli Incident.* Astro-Media Corp., 1976.

Ellis, Normandi. *Awakening Osiris: The Egyptian Book of the Dead.* Phanes Press, 1988.

Fix, William R. *Star Maps.* Octopus Books, 1979.

Freer, Neil. *Breaking the Godspell.* Falcon Press, 1987.

Fuller, John G. *The Interrupted Journey.* The Dial Press, 1966.

Grant, Joan. *Eyes of Horus.* Ariel Press, 1942.

Hart, George. *Dictionary of Egyptian Gods and Goddesses.* Routledge & Kegan Paul, 1986.

Jung, Carl. *Man and His Symbols.* Dell Publishing, 1964.

Krupp, E.C. *Echoes of the Ancient Skies: The Astronomy of Lost Civilizations.* New American Library, 1983.

McConnell, James V. *Understanding Human Behavior, Second Edition.* Holt, Rinehart & Winston, 1977.

Moody, Raymond. *Life After Life.* Stackpole Books, 1976.

Sitchin, Zecharia. *The Stairway to Heaven.* Avon Books, 1985.

Sitchin, Zecharia. *The Twelfth Planet.* Avon Books, 1976.

Sitchin, Zecharia. *The Wars of Gods and Men.* Avon Books, 1985.

Strieber, Whitley. *Communion.* William Morrow, 1987.

Temple, Robert K.G. *The Sirius Mystery.* Destiny Books, 1976.

Wolkstein, D. and Kramer, S.N. *Inanna: Queen of Heaven and Earth.* Harper and Row, 1983.

Wood, David. *Genisis: The First Book of Revelations.* The Baton Press, 1985.

Zeilik, Michael. *Astronomy: The Evolving Universe.* Harper & Row, 1979.

New American Standard Bible. Thomas Nelson Publishers, 1960.

Holy Bible, New International Version. Zondervaan Publishers, 1978.

The Living Webster Encyclopedic Dictionary of the English Language. English Language Institute of America, 1977.

About the Authors

Lyssa Royal holds a B.A. in Psychology and is a nationally known channel and lecturer residing in Sedona, Arizona. In 1979 she had a clear UFO sighting witnessed by her family which triggered a profound interest in the extraterrestrial phenomenon. Being inspired by Darryl Anka and Bashar, Lyssa began a search for answers concerning Earth's connection with other civilizations. She diligently honed her channeling skills and began to receive information which, through research, was later confirmed by independent sources. She continues to channel and lecture, and has been seen on national and international television as well as in national magazine publications. Though she works quite often with extraterrestrial information, the practical applications of what she teaches and channels is of utmost priority to her.

Keith Priest is an independent researcher and sculptor living in Sedona Arizona. He studied Music at Michigan State University, majoring in Piano Technology and Historical Tuning Systems. Keith's life philosophy has always been to ask, "Why?" His interest in the extraterrestrial issue was triggered in the early 1980s thru the channelings of Darryl Anka and Bashar. Through his research he has delved into Ancient Languages, Biblical studies, Anthropology, Archaeology, History, and Religions, combining those studies with astronomy, Mythology, and psychology. Though he has never even seen a UFO much less an extraterrestrial, his studies have shown him that the E.T. issue not only fits nicely into all these areas but in fact is an integral piece of the puzzle that may connect them all.